McGRAW-HILL READING

Spelling

Grade 3

Practice Book

McGraw-Hill School Division

New York   Farmington

CONTENTS

Book 3.1/Unit 1

McGraw-Hill School Division

Book 3.1/Unit 2

McGraw-Hill School Division

Book 3.1/Unit 3

McGraw-Hill School Division

Book 3.2 / Unit 1

McGraw-Hill School Division

Book 3.2 / Unit 2

McGraw-Hill School Division

Book 3.2/Unit 3

McGraw-Hill School Division

Words with Short Vowels

Pretest Directions

Fold back the paper along the dotted line. Use the blanks to write each word as it is read aloud. When you finish the test, unfold the paper. Use the list at the right to correct any spelling mistakes. Practice the words you missed for the Posttest.

To Parents

Here are the results of your child's weekly spelling Pretest. You can help your child study for the Posttest by following these simple steps for each word on the word list:

1. Read the word to your child.

2. Have your child write the word, saying each letter as it is written.

3. Say each letter of the word as your child checks the spelling.

4. If a mistake has been made, have your child read each letter of the correctly spelled word aloud, and then repeat steps 1-3.

1. _____	1. leg
2. _____	2. black
3. _____	3. much
4. _____	4. bag
5. _____	5. rocks
6. _____	6. kept
7. _____	7. hid
8. _____	8. window
9. _____	9. van
10. _____	10. mix
11. _____	11. rub
12. _____	12. ever
13. _____	13. buzz
14. _____	14. body
15. _____	15. thing

Challenge Words

_____	astonished
_____	enormous
_____	journey
_____	scattered
_____	surrounded

Words with Short Vowels

Using the Word Study Steps

1. LOOK at the word.
2. SAY the word aloud.
3. STUDY the letters in the word.
4. WRITE the word.
5. CHECK the word.
   Did you spell the word right?
   If not, go back to step 1.

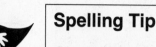

| **Spelling Tip** |
| Short vowel sounds are usually spelled with one letter. |
| Examples: |
| b**e**g   s**a**g   l**i**d |

Find Rhyming Words

Circle the word in each row that rhymes with the word in dark type.

1.	**beg**	rag	leg	bog
2.	**rack**	sick	block	black
3.	**such**	each	much	lunch
4.	**sag**	sat	big	bag
5.	**clocks**	rocks	cracks	clucks
6.	**wept**	wiped	left	kept
7.	**lid**	lad	lied	hid
8.	**window**	doe	do	drew
9.	**man**	men	van	vend
10.	**six**	sit	box	mix
11.	**scrub**	rub	rob	describe
12.	**clever**	deer	ever	clover
13.	**fuzz**	furs	fizz	buzz
14.	**anybody**	body	copy	anyone
15.	**ring**	rang	thing	clung

To Parents or Helpers:

Using the Word Study Steps above as your child comes across any new words will help him or her spell well. Review the steps as you both go over this week's spelling words.

Go over the Spelling Tip with your child. Ask him or her to find words with short vowel sounds and point out the letter that makes the vowel sound in each word. Help your child complete the spelling activity.

McGraw-Hill School Division

● ## Words with Short Vowels

leg	bag	hid	mix	buzz
black	rocks	window	rub	body
much	kept	van	ever	thing

Rhyme Time

Write the spelling words that rhyme with the words below. Then circle the letter that spells the short-vowel sound in each word.

1. did _____

2. slept _____

3. fix _____

4. fuzz _____

5. peg _____

6. swing _____

7. tag _____

8. shrub _____

9. tack _____

10. can _____

Vowel Power

Write the spelling words that contain each short vowel sound below.

Short a

11. _____ **12.** _____ **13.** _____

Short e

14. _____ **15.** _____ **16.** _____

Short i

17. _____ **18.** _____ **19.** _____

20. _____

Short o

21. _____ **22.** _____

Short u

23. _____ **24.** _____ **25.** _____

Words with Short Vowels

leg	bag	hid	mix	buzz
black	rocks	window	rub	body
much	kept	van	ever	thing

What's the Word?

Complete each sentence with a spelling word.

1. The _____ spider crawled slowly along the wall.

2. Crickets _____ their front wings together to chirp.

3. The humming sound of a bee is a _____.

4. Dad hurt his _____ and could not walk.

5. When our dog _____ the bone, I found it under a pillow.

6. I opened a _____ of chips for the party.

7. I can't do one more _____ today.

8. The dress didn't fit the doll's _____.

9. Mom _____ our drawings in a box.

10. We washed the _____ with a glass cleaner.

Define It!

Write the spelling words that have the same meanings as the words or phrases below.

11. a kind of truck _____   14. stir together _____

12. always _____   15. stones _____

13. a great amount _____

Challenge Extension: Ask students to write a "fill in the blank" sentence for each Challenge Word and then exchange papers with a partner to complete the sentences.

McGraw-Hill School Division

Words with Short Vowels

Proofreading

There are six spelling mistakes in this visitor's guide to the zoo. Circle the misspelled words. Write the words correctly on the lines below.

A zoo is a winndow to the animal kingdom. If you wonder how wild animals live, visit the zoo. Come by bus, car, vann, or train. Remember this: these animals are not pets.

Follow these safety rules. Don't throw roks at the birds. Don't put your arm or legg through a bar of a cage. A dangerous animal might be cept there. Don't pet the animals.

There is a lot you can do at the zoo. Watch the seals play in the water. See a blak bear. Have fun!

1._____ 2._____ 3._____

4._____ 5._____ 6._____

Writing Activity

Write a postcard to a friend describing the zoo. Use at least four spelling words in your description.

_____

_____

_____

_____

_____

_____

McGraw-Hill School Division

Words with Long *a* and Long *e*

Pretest Directions

Fold back the paper along the dotted line. Use the blanks to write each word as it is read aloud. When you finish the test, unfold the paper. Use the list at the right to correct any spelling mistakes. Practice the words you missed for the Posttest.

To Parents

Here are the results of your child's weekly spelling Pretest. You can help your child study for the Posttest by following these simple steps for each word on the word list:

1. Read the word to your child.

2. Have your child write the word, saying each letter as it is written.

3. Say each letter of the word as your child checks the spelling.

4. If a mistake has been made, have your child read each letter of the correctly spelled word aloud, and then repeat steps 1-3.

1. _____
2. _____
3. _____
4. _____
5. _____
6. _____
7. _____
8. _____
9. _____
10. _____
11. _____
12. _____
13. _____
14. _____
15. _____

1. plane
2. team
3. raise
4. breeze
5. paper
6. marry
7. weigh
8. thief
9. cream
10. awake
11. grade
12. creek
13. carry
14. sail
15. neighbor

Challenge Words

_____ continue

_____ correct

_____ embarrass

_____ legend

_____ unusual

McGraw-Hill School Division

Name_____ Date_____

Words with Long *a* and Long *e*

Using the Word Study Steps

1. LOOK at the word.

2. SAY the word aloud.

3. STUDY the letters in the word.

4. WRITE the word.

5. CHECK the word.
   Did you spell the word right?
   If not, go back to step 1.

Spelling Tip

Words with **i** and **e** can be tricky. This rhyme gives a tip.

i before **e**

except after **c**

or when sounded like /a/

as in neighbor and weigh

Crossword Puzzle

Solve the crossword puzzle with spelling words that complete the sentences.

ACROSS

2. You need a pen and ____ to draw.
3. He plays on the baseball ____ .
5. I'm wide ____ after my nap.
6. The flag blew in the ____ .
7. Did you get a good ____ on the test?
11. He will ____ his boat on the lake.
12. My next door ____ is coming over.
13. I help Mom ____ the heavy bags.

DOWN

1. The water in the ____ is cold.
2. The pilot flew the ____ .
3. The ____ stole her purse.
4. I'll have a big wedding when I ____ .
8. I ____ ninety pounds.
9. Do you like ____ in your coffee?
10. I will ____ my right hand to answer.

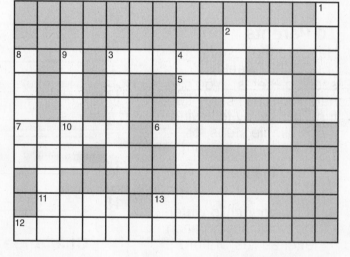

To Parents or Helpers:
Using the Word Study Steps above as your child comes across any new words will help him or her spell well. Review the steps as you both go over this week's spelling words.
Go over the Spelling Tip with your child. Help him or her find other words that contain i and e. Use the rhyme to explain the spelling pattern.
Help your child complete the spelling activity.

Book 3.1/Unit 1 | 15
Phoebe and the Spelling Bee

McGraw-Hill School Division

Words with Long *a* and Long *e*

plane	breeze	weigh	awake	carry
team	paper	thief	grade	sail
raise	marry	cream	creek	neighbor

Write the spelling words that contain the matching spelling of the long **a** sound.

long *a* spelled *a*

1. _____

long *a* spelled *a-e*

4. _____

5. _____

6. _____

long *a* spelled *ai*

2. _____

3. _____

long *a* spelled *eigh*

7. _____

8. _____

Write the spelling words that contain the matching spelling of the long **e** sound.

long *e* spelled e*a*

9. _____

10. _____

long *e* spelled *y*

13. _____

14. _____

long *e* spelled *ee*

11. _____

12. _____

long *a* spelled *eigh*

15. _____

Words with Long a [and Long e]

plane		awake	carry
team		grade	sail
raise		creek	neighbor

[handwritten note overlapping: Words with Long a and Long E]

It Takes Three

Write a spelling [word that goes with] the other two words.

1. group, club, _____ **2.** river, pond, _____

3. robber, crook, _____ **4.** measure, balance, _____

What Does It Mean?

Write a spelling word that matches each clue below.

5. Not asleep _____

6. A flying machine _____

7. Thin sheet used for writing _____

8. The person who lives next door _____

9. A class or year in school _____

10. Heavy, thick milk _____

11. A gentle wind _____

Past Tense

To form the past tense of a verb you usually add *-ed* . If there is a y at the end of the word, it changes to *i*. If there is an *e* at the end it is dropped. Put these words in the past tense:

12. raise _____ **13.** marry _____

14. sail _____ **15.** carry _____

Challenge Extension: Have students draw a picture to illustrate each Challenge Word, then exchange papers with a partner and label each other's pictures.

McGraw-Hill School Division

Words with Long *a* and Long *e*

Proofreading

There are six spelling mistakes in this letter. Circle the misspelled words. Write the words correctly on the lines below.

Dear Laura,

Our camping trip was so much fun. We fished in a creak. I caught a fish but let it go. Mom said that the fish didn't whay enough.

We all worked as a teem. Everyone helped to put up the tents. I also helped raze the sail on the rented boat.

The first night, I lay awayk watching the stars. We went on hikes, but I didn't like to cary my own backpack.

Write soon!
Your friend,
Melissa

1. _____   2. _____

3. _____   4. _____

5. _____   6. _____

Writing Activity

Write a letter to a friend describing a fun event. Use at least four spelling words in your description.

_____

_____

_____

_____

Words with Long *a* and Long *e*

Look at the words in each set. One word in each set is spelled correctly.
Use a pencil to color in the circle in front of that word. Before you begin,
look at the sample sets of words. Sample A has been done for you.
Do Sample B by yourself. When you are sure you know what to do,
you may go on with the rest of the page.

Sample A
- Ⓐ trail
- Ⓑ trayl
- Ⓒ trayle
- Ⓓ treil

Sample B
- Ⓔ sneze
- Ⓕ sneez
- Ⓖ sneeze
- Ⓗ sneaze

1. Ⓐ marry
   Ⓑ marrie
   Ⓒ mairy
   Ⓓ mary

2. Ⓔ plaen
   Ⓕ playne
   Ⓖ playn
   Ⓗ plane

3. Ⓐ teim
   Ⓑ teem
   Ⓒ team
   Ⓓ tiem

4. Ⓔ karry
   Ⓕ carry
   Ⓖ cary
   Ⓗ kerry

5. Ⓐ sail
   Ⓑ sayle
   Ⓒ saile
   Ⓓ sael

6. Ⓔ paper
   Ⓕ payper
   Ⓖ paiper
   Ⓗ peighper

7. Ⓐ grayde
   Ⓑ graide
   Ⓒ grade
   Ⓓ grayed

8. Ⓔ raze
   Ⓕ raize
   Ⓖ rays
   Ⓗ raise

9. Ⓐ naybur
   Ⓑ neighbor
   Ⓒ naybor
   Ⓓ neighber

10. Ⓔ cream
    Ⓕ creem
    Ⓖ kream
    Ⓗ kreme

11. Ⓐ weigh
    Ⓑ wiegh
    Ⓒ wey
    Ⓓ whay

12. Ⓔ thiefe
    Ⓕ theef
    Ⓖ thief
    Ⓗ theif

13. Ⓐ awake
    Ⓑ awayke
    Ⓒ aweighke
    Ⓓ awaik

14. Ⓔ creak
    Ⓕ creek
    Ⓖ criek
    Ⓗ creack

15. Ⓐ briexe
    Ⓑ brieze
    Ⓒ breze
    Ⓓ breeze

Words with Long *i* and Long *o*

Pretest Directions

Fold back the paper along the dotted line. Use the blanks to write each word as it is read aloud. When you finish the test, unfold the paper. Use the list at the right to correct any spelling mistakes. Practice the words you missed for the Posttest.

To Parents

Here are the results of your child's weekly spelling Pretest. You can help your child study for the Posttest by following these simple steps for each word on the word list:

1. Read the word to your child.

2. Have your child write the word, saying each letter as it is written.

3. Say each letter of the word as your child checks the spelling.

4. If a mistake has been made, have your child read each letter of the correctly spelled word aloud, and then repeat steps 1-3.

1. _____	1. might
2. _____	2. life
3. _____	3. rode
4. _____	4. own
5. _____	5. most
6. _____	6. tie
7. _____	7. find
8. _____	8. toast
9. _____	9. wipe
10. _____	10. flight
11. _____	11. bicycle
12. _____	12. lie
13. _____	13. spoke
14. _____	14. ago
15. _____	15. thrown

Challenge Words

_____ guard

_____ length

_____ royal

_____ straighten

_____ within

Words with Long *i* and Long *o*

Using the Word Study Steps

1. LOOK at the word.

2. SAY the word aloud.

3. STUDY the letters in the word.

4. WRITE the word.

5. CHECK the word.
   Did you spell the word right?
   If not, go back to step 1.

Spelling Tip

When there is a long vowel sound at the beginning or in the middle of a one syllable word, it usually has two vowels. How many spelling words follow this rule?

life **ow**n **to**ast

Find and Circle

Where are the spelling words?

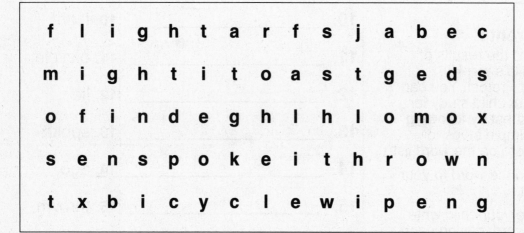

```
f  l  i  g  h  t  a  r  f  s  j  a  b  e  c
m  i  g  h  t  i  t  o  a  s  t  g  e  d  s
o  f  i  n  d  e  g  h  l  h  l  o  m  o  x
s  e  n  s  p  o  k  e  i  t  h  r  o  w  n
t  x  b  i  c  y  c  l  e  w  i  p  e  n  g
```

To Parents or Helpers:
    Using the Word Study Steps above as your child comes across any new words will help him or her spell well. Review the steps as you both go over this week's spelling words.
    Go over the Spelling Tip with your child. Ask if he or she knows other one syllable words that contain two vowels. Help your child find and circle the spelling words in the puzzle.

McGraw-Hill School Division

Words with Long *a* and Long *e*

plane	breeze	weigh	awake	carry
team	paper	thief	grade	sail
raise	marry	cream	creek	neighbor

Write the spelling words that contain the matching spelling of the long **a** sound.

long *a* spelled *a*

1. _____

long *a* spelled *a-e*

4. _____

5. _____

6. _____

long *a* spelled *ai*

2. _____

3. _____

long *a* spelled *eigh*

7. _____

8. _____

Write the spelling words that contain the matching spelling of the long **e** sound.

long *e* spelled e*a*

9. _____

10. _____

long *e* spelled *y*

13. _____

14. _____

long *e* spelled *ee*

11. _____

12. _____

long *a* spelled *eigh*

15. _____

Words with Long *a* and Long *e*

plane	breeze	weigh	awake	carry
team	paper	thief	grade	sail
raise	marry	cream	creek	neighbor

It Takes Three

Write a spelling word that goes with the other two words.

1. group, club, _____ **2.** river, pond, _____

3. robber, crook, _____ **4.** measure, balance, _____

What Does It Mean?

Write a spelling word that matches each clue below.

5. Not asleep _____

6. A flying machine _____

7. Thin sheet used for writing _____

8. The person who lives next door _____

9. A class or year in school _____

10. Heavy, thick milk _____

11. A gentle wind _____

Past Tense

To form the past tense of a verb you usually add *-ed* . If there is a y at the end of the word, it changes to *i*. If there is an *e* at the end it is dropped. Put these words in the past tense:

12. raise _____ **13.** marry _____

14. sail _____ **15.** carry _____

Challenge Extension: Have students draw a picture to illustrate each Challenge Word, then exchange papers with a partner and label each other's pictures.

Book 3.1/Unit 1
Phoebe and the Spelling Bee 15

McGraw-Hill School Division

Words with Long *i* and Long *o*

might	own	find	flight	spoke
life	most	toast	bicycle	ago
rode	tie	wipe	lie	thrown

Pattern Power!

Write the spelling words from the box that have the long **i** sound spelled with the letters below.

i - e

1. _____

2. _____

i

3. _____

4. _____

igh

5. _____

6. _____

ie

7. _____

8. _____

Write the words from the box that have the long **o** sound spelled with the letters below.

o - e

9. _____

10. _____

ow

11. _____

12. _____

o

13. _____

14. _____

oa

15. _____

Words Within Words

Write the spelling words in which each of the words below can be found.

16. rod _____

17. light _____

18. cycle _____

19. go _____

20. row _____

Words with Long *i* and Long *o*

might	own	find	flight	spoke
life	most	toast	bicycle	ago
rode	tie	wipe	lie	thrown

Words in Sentences

Write a spelling word to complete each sentence.

1. A _____ has two wheels and handle bars.

2. Long _____, dinosaurs roamed the Earth.

3. I _____ go to camp this summer for two weeks.

4. Did Bobby have one or two slices of _____ for breakfast?

5. _____ your muddy shoes on the doormat!

6. The ball was _____ ten feet into the air.

7. Our teacher _____ in a low voice.

8. This building has only one _____ of stairs.

9. Stacy _____ to school in a bus last year.

10. Many people who live in the city don't _____ a car.

11. If you don't _____ your shoelaces, you'll trip over them.

12. We read a book about the long _____ of Benjamin Franklin.

Opposites

Write the spelling word from the box that is
the antonym, or opposite, of each word below.

lie	find	most	tie

13. fewest _____

14. lose _____

15. truth _____

16. untie _____

Challenge Extension: For each Challenge Word, have
students find and write out a sentence in the selection
in which the word appears.

Book 3.1/Unit 1
Opt: An Illusionary Tale

16

McGraw-Hill School Division

Words with Long *i* and Long *o*

Proofreading

There are six spelling mistakes in this paragraph. Circle the misspelled words. Write the words correctly on the lines below.

Many years agow, the Wright brothers lived in Dayton, Ohio. Orville and Wilbur Wright were inventors. They used their bysickle shop to build the first airplane. First they did tests with kites to see if their idea mite work. Then they did flite tests on gliders in Kitty Hawk, North Carolina. When the brothers couldn't fynd anyone to make an engine for their plane, they built one themselves. Finally, in 1903, Orville Wright flew the first plane that had an engine and a propeller. No one else rowd with him, not even his brother.

1. _____ 2. _____ 3. _____

4. _____ 5. _____ 6. _____

Writing Activity

Imagine that you have your own bicycle shop. Write how you manage the shop. Use at least four spelling words in your explanation.

_____

_____

_____

_____

_____

Words with Long *i* and Long *o*

Look at the words in each set. One word in each set is spelled correctly.
Use a pencil to color in the circle in front of that word. Before you begin,
look at the sample sets of words. Sample A has been done for you.
Do Sample B by yourself. When you are sure you know what to do,
you may go on with the rest of the page.

Sample A
(A) cind
(B) kind
(C) kynd
(D) kinde

Sample B
(E) light
(F) lite
(G) liet
(H) lygte

1. (A) spoak
   (B) spowke
   (C) spok
   (D) spoke

2. (E) aggo
   (F) agow
   (G) ago
   (H) ugo

3. (A) might
   (B) miht
   (C) mighte
   (D) mitte

4. (E) tost
   (F) toast
   (G) towst
   (H) toste

5. (A) fighnd
   (B) finde
   (C) fynd
   (D) find

6. (E) bycycle
   (F) bisickal
   (G) bicycle
   (H) bysikel

7. (A) lie
   (B) li
   (C) luy
   (D) ligh

8. (E) flite
   (F) flight
   (G) flyt
   (H) fligt

9. (A) own
   (B) oan
   (C) owne
   (D) ohn

10. (E) liffe
    (F) lyff
    (G) life
    (H) ligh

11. (A) tye
    (B) ty
    (C) tie
    (D) ti

12. (E) rowd
    (F) rode
    (G) roade
    (H) rodde

13. (A) throne
    (B) thrown
    (C) trone
    (D) throan

14. (E) whipe
    (F) wype
    (G) wiep
    (H) wipe

15. (A) mose
    (B) moaste
    (C) most
    (D) mowst

Words with /û/ and /ü/

Pretest Directions

Fold back the paper along the dotted line. Use the blanks to write each word as it is read aloud. When you finish the test, unfold the paper. Use the list at the right to correct any spelling mistakes. Practice the words you missed for the Posttest.

To Parents

Here are the results of your child's weekly spelling Pretest. You can help your child study for the Posttest by following these simple steps for each word on the word list:

1. Read the word to your child.

2. Have your child write the word, saying each letter as it is written.

3. Say each letter of the word as your child checks the spelling.

4. If a mistake has been made, have your child read each letter of the correctly spelled word aloud, and then repeat steps 1-3.

1. _____ 1. music
2. _____ 2. broom
3. _____ 3. soup
4. _____ 4. fruit
5. _____ 5. huge
6. _____ 6. drew
7. _____ 7. truth
8. _____ 8. pool
9. _____ 9. goose
10. _____ 10. excuse
11. _____ 11. dew
12. _____ 12. juice
13. _____ 13. crew
14. _____ 14. group
15. _____ 15. produce

Challenge Words

_____ ceiling
_____ eager
_____ including
_____ scene
_____ section

Words with /û/ and /ü/

Using the Word Study Steps

1. LOOK at the word.

2. SAY the word aloud.

3. STUDY the letters in the word.

4. WRITE the word.

5. CHECK the word.
Did you spell the word right?
If not, go back to step 1.

Spelling Tip

Make up clues to help you remember the spelling.

(**u** and **i** love fr**ui**t)

Word Scramble

Unscramble each set of letters to make a spelling word.

1. csium _____

2. wred _____

3. ewd _____

4. morbo _____

5. tuhtr _____

6. cueji _____

7. opsu _____

8. olop _____

9. wcre _____

10. fitur _____

11. soeog _____

12. pugro _____

13. gueh _____

14. suxcee _____

15. ecrudpo _____

To Parents or Helpers:

Using the Word Study Steps above as your child comes across any new words will help him or her spell well. Review the steps as you both go over this week's spelling words.

Go over the Spelling Tip with your child. Ask your child if he or she knows other words that clues can be used to remember spelling. Help him or her write the words with clues to remember spelling .

Help your child unscramble the spelling words.

McGraw-Hill School Division

Words with /û/ and /ü/

music	fruit	truth	excuse	crew
broom	huge	pool	dew	group
soup	drew	goose	juice	produce

Word Sort

Fill in the blanks with the words that have the long **u** sound spelled with the letters shown.

u -e

1. _____

2. _____

3. _____

4. _____

5. _____

6. _____

ew

7. _____

8. _____

9. _____

ui

10. _____

11. _____

ou

12. _____

13. _____

u

14. _____

15. _____

Unscramble It

Unscramble each spelling word below and write it correctly on the line.

16. eguh _____

17. cumis _____

18. tuifr _____

Words with /û/ and /ü/

music	fruit	truth	excuse	crew
broom	huge	pool	dew	group
soup	drew	goose	juice	produce

Analogies

An **analogy** is a statement that compares sets of words that are alike in some way: *Night* is to *day* as *black* is to *white*. This analogy points out that *night* and *day* are opposite in the same way that *black* and *white* are opposite.

Use spelling words to complete the analogies below.

1. *On* is to *off* as *tiny* is to _____.

2. *Wet* is to *dry* as *lie* is to _____.

3. *TV* is to *picture* as *radio* is to _____.

4. *Carrot* is to *vegetable* as *apple* is to _____.

5. *Peanut* is to *peanut butter* as *orange*

   is to *orange* _____.

In the Dictionary

Many dictionary entries have sample sentences that show how the word can be used. Complete each sample sentence with a spelling word.

6. The artist _____ a picture of a garden.

7. Do you like to swim in a _____ or in the ocean?

8. Use a _____ to sweep the floor.

9. Give a good reason or an _____ for your lateness.

10. Some companies _____ parts for cars.

Challenge Extension: Write the Challenge Words on the board in scrambled order and ask students to students to write them in ABC order.

Book 3.1/Unit 1
Max Malone 10

McGraw-Hill School Division

Words with /û/ and /ü/

Proofreading

There are five spelling mistakes in the fairy tale. Circle the misspelled words. Write the words correctly on the lines below.

When the mewzik started, a very strange thing happened. A picture in the fairy tale book came to life. It was amazing. First, a guce stepped out from the page. Then a groop of chicks from the picture came out and sat around it in a circle.

What do you think happened next?

Well, the chicks began to sing and dance. Suddenly, a parade of froot marched across the page. What a silly sight to see bananas, oranges, and pears marching!

Finally, the record stopped playing. Of course, everyone stopped dancing, singing, and marching. And that's the truthe!

1. _____ 2. _____ 3. _____

4. _____ 5. _____

Writing Activity

Write a list of amazing things that could happen in your own fairy tale. Use at least five spelling words.

_____

_____

_____

_____

_____

McGraw-Hill School Division

Words with /û/ and /ü/

Look at the words in each set. One word in each set is spelled correctly.
Use a pencil to color in the circle in front of that word. Before you begin,
look at the sample sets of words. Sample A has been done for you.
Do Sample B by yourself. When you are sure you know what to do,
you may go on with the rest of the page.

Sample A
- (A) klock
- (B) clock
- (C) clok
- (D) clawk

Sample B
- (E) houp
- (F) hoop
- (G) hewp
- (H) hoope

1.
- (A) soup
- (B) sewp
- (C) soop
- (D) soope

2.
- (E) guce
- (F) goose
- (G) gewse
- (H) goos

3.
- (A) hewg
- (B) hooge
- (C) huje
- (D) huge

4.
- (E) croo
- (F) crewe
- (G) crew
- (H) crue

5.
- (A) pool
- (B) pewl
- (C) pule
- (D) poole

6.
- (E) jooce
- (F) juice
- (G) juce
- (H) juise

7.
- (A) prodoose
- (B) pruduce
- (C) produce
- (D) produse

8.
- (E) grupe
- (F) group
- (G) grewp
- (H) groop

9.
- (A) excuse
- (B) excoose
- (C) egscuse
- (D) excewse

10.
- (E) truthe
- (F) trewth
- (G) truth
- (H) trooth

11.
- (A) fruit
- (B) froot
- (C) frute
- (D) frewt

12.
- (E) brume
- (F) broome
- (G) broom
- (H) brewme

13.
- (A) drue
- (B) drewe
- (C) drew
- (D) droo

14.
- (E) music
- (F) mewzik
- (G) musik
- (H) muzik

15.
- (A) dou
- (B) doo
- (C) dewe
- (D) dew

Words from Physical Education

Pretest Directions

Fold back the paper along the dotted line. Use the blanks to write each word as it is read aloud. When you finish the test, unfold the paper. Use the list at the right to correct any spelling mistakes. Practice the words you missed for the Posttest.

To Parents

Here are the results of your child's weekly spelling Pretest. You can help your child study for the Posttest by following these simple steps for each word on the word list:

1. Read the word to your child.

2. Have your child write the word, saying each letter as it is written.

3. Say each letter of the word as your child checks the spelling.

4. If a mistake has been made, have your child read each letter of the correctly spelled word aloud, and then repeat steps 1-3.

1. _____	1. player
2. _____	2. strike
3. _____	3. parade
4. _____	4. mitt
5. _____	5. batter
6. _____	6. bases
7. _____	7. glove
8. _____	8. action
9. _____	9. crowd
10. _____	10. baseball
11. _____	11. mound
12. _____	12. season
13. _____	13. foul
14. _____	14. outfield
15. _____	15. record

Challenge Words

_____ celebrated

_____ cork

_____ pitcher

_____ score

_____ wrap

Words from Physical Education

Using the Word Study Steps

1. LOOK at the word.

2. SAY the word aloud.

3. STUDY the letters in the word.

4. WRITE the word.

5. CHECK the word.
   Did you spell the word right?
   If not, go back to step 1.

Spelling Tip

Look for word chunks or smaller words that help you remember the spelling of the word.

play + er = player

base + ball = baseball

Find and Circle

Where are the spelling words?

e	p	l	a	y	e	r	s	t	r	i	k	e	a	f	b	g	c
m	p	a	r	a	d	e	r	e	c	o	r	d	b	o	a	l	r
i	s	e	a	s	o	n	b	a	t	t	e	r	c	u	s	o	o
t	o	u	t	f	i	e	l	d	m	o	u	n	d	l	e	v	w
t	b	a	s	e	b	a	l	l	a	c	t	i	o	n	s	e	d

To Parents or Helpers:

Using the Word Study Steps above as your child comes across any new words will help him or her spell well. Review the steps as you both go over this weekís spelling words.

Go over the Spelling Tip with your child. Ask him or her to find helpful chunks or smaller words in other new words. Help your child find and circle the spelling words in the puzzle.

Words from Physical Education

player	mitt	glove	baseball	foul
strike	batter	action	mound	outfield
parade	bases	crowd	season	record

Rhyme Time

Write the one-syllable spelling word that rhymes with each of these words.

[handwritten note covering part of page: front and Back please]

1. bike _____

3. love _____

5. howl _____   **6.** loud _____

Write the two-syllable spelling words that rhyme with the words below.

7. mayor _____   **8.** vases _____

9. charade_____   **10.** traction _____

11. matter _____   **12.** reason _____

Find Spelling Words

Find six spelling words in the paragraph. Write each word on the line.

> A batter hit the ball during a baseball game. The ball got stuck in the muddy outfield. No one could find it. The player ran around the bases and reached home. The hit broke a record. It was the shortest home run in history.

13. _____   **14.** _____   **15.** _____

16. _____   **17.** _____   **18.** _____

Words from Physical Education

player	mitt	glove	baseball	foul
strike	batter	action	mound	outfield
parade	bases	crowd	season	record

What Am I?
Write the spelling list word that matches each clue.

1. I'm played with bases, a ball, and a bat. _____

2. I'm summer, fall winter, or spring. _____

3. I'm a special type of glove. _____

4. I'm where the pitcher stands. _____

5. I've got marchers, and people watch me. _____

6. I keep your hand warm. _____

7. I'm a ball hit out of play. _____

8. You'd like to break me. _____

9. I hit the balls, catch them, and run. _____

10. If the games exciting, there's lots of me. _____

Words in Sentences
Decide which list word fits in each sentence. Write the missing letters.

11. Mickey Mantle played center position in the _____.

12. Babe Ruth was a great home-run _____.

13. If you swing at the ball and miss, it is called a _____.

14. After she hit the ball, Kathy ran around the _____.

15. Then the _____ in the ball park shouted "Hooray!"

Word Journal
One of your list words is *baseball*. How would you explain the game of baseball to a friend? Write some of the rules below. Use at least three spelling words and circle them.

_____

_____

_____

Challenge Extension: Have students write a sentence for each Challenge Word.

McGraw-Hill School Division

Words from Physical Education

Proofreading

There are six spelling mistakes in this paragraph. Circle the misspelled words. Write the words correctly on the lines below.

It was too hot to play basebal, but we did anyway. Joey was the first battir. The pitcher dug her heels in and threw the ball hard. Joey swung and missed.

"Stryke one!" the umpire called.

On the next pitch, Joey hit the ball hard. However, the ball popped up in the air behind him. "Foule ball!" cried the umpire. The third time, Joey swung at the ball again. This time he hit the ball over the wall in the outfeeld.

"This is one for the rekerd books," said our coach.

1. _____ 2. _____ 3. _____

4. _____ 5. _____ 6. _____

Writing Activity

Write a short story about a baseball game. It can be about a real game or one that you make up. Use at least four list words in your story.

_____

_____

_____

_____

McGraw-Hill School Division

Words from Physical Education

Look at the words in each set. One word in each set is spelled correctly.
Use a pencil to color in the circle in front of that word. Before you begin,
look at the sample sets of words. Sample A has been done for you.
Do Sample B by yourself. When you are sure you know what to do,
you may go on with the rest of the page.

Sample A
- Ⓐ bal
- Ⓑ baul
- ⬤ ball
- Ⓓ balle

Sample B
- Ⓔ base
- Ⓕ bas
- Ⓖ bace
- Ⓗ bayse

1.
- Ⓐ player
- Ⓑ playar
- Ⓒ playre
- Ⓓ playyer

2.
- Ⓔ glov
- Ⓕ glouve
- Ⓖ glove
- Ⓗ gluve

3.
- Ⓐ foule
- Ⓑ foul
- Ⓒ fowel
- Ⓓ faul

4.
- Ⓔ mownd
- Ⓕ mounde
- Ⓖ mound
- Ⓗ moud

5.
- Ⓐ stoke
- Ⓑ strike
- Ⓒ strik
- Ⓓ strice

6.
- Ⓔ aktion
- Ⓕ acshun
- Ⓖ akschune
- Ⓗ action

7.
- Ⓐ baseball
- Ⓑ basball
- Ⓒ basebal
- Ⓓ bacebaul

8.
- Ⓔ buter
- Ⓕ batter
- Ⓖ battur
- Ⓗ battir

9.
- Ⓐ ceazon
- Ⓑ seeson
- Ⓒ season
- Ⓓ seasen

10.
- Ⓔ bases
- Ⓕ bayses
- Ⓖ baces
- Ⓗ basuz

11.
- Ⓐ rekord
- Ⓑ record
- Ⓒ recorde
- Ⓓ ricord

12.
- Ⓔ mit
- Ⓕ mitte
- Ⓖ mitt
- Ⓗ muit

13.
- Ⓐ owtfield
- Ⓑ outfeald
- Ⓒ outfeild
- Ⓓ outfield

14.
- Ⓔ crowd
- Ⓕ croud
- Ⓖ crod
- Ⓗ krowd

15.
- Ⓐ perade
- Ⓑ parad
- Ⓒ parade
- Ⓓ pirayd

Book 3.1/Unit 1
Champions of the World

Book 3.1/Unit 1 Review Test

Read each sentence. If an underlined word is spelled wrong, fill in the circle that goes with that word. If no word is spelled wrong, fill in the circle below NONE. Read Sample A, and do Sample B.

A. I <u>like</u> the <u>nayght</u> <u>owl</u> in the room.
     A   B   C

                                NONE
A. Ⓐ   Ⓑ   Ⓒ   ⬤(D)

B. Her <u>brume</u> was <u>thrown</u> on the <u>rocks</u>.
       E   F   G

                                NONE
B. Ⓔ   Ⓕ   Ⓖ   Ⓗ

1. I <u>might</u> see the <u>parade</u> on my <u>bicycle</u>.
      A   B   C

                                NONE
1. Ⓐ   Ⓑ   Ⓒ   Ⓓ

2. They <u>strike</u> <u>truth</u> from the <u>record</u>.
        E   F   G

                                NONE
2. Ⓔ   Ⓕ   Ⓖ   Ⓗ

3. A good <u>thief</u> <u>might</u> not tell the <u>trueth</u>.
          A   B   C

                                NONE
3. Ⓐ   Ⓑ   Ⓒ   Ⓓ

4. The <u>black</u> <u>toast</u> is on the <u>paper</u>.
       E   F   G

                                NONE
4. Ⓔ   Ⓕ   Ⓖ   Ⓗ

5. She wore that <u>glove</u> to a <u>parade</u> a long time <u>ago</u>.
               A   B   C

                                NONE
5. Ⓐ   Ⓑ   Ⓒ   Ⓓ

6. Does the <u>rock</u> <u>whay</u> more than the <u>paper</u>?
           E   F   G

                                NONE
6. Ⓔ   Ⓕ   Ⓖ   Ⓗ

7. The <u>thief</u> will <u>rubb</u> the <u>rocks</u> for luck.
       A   B   C

                                NONE
7. Ⓐ   Ⓑ   Ⓒ   Ⓓ

8. I will <u>rub</u> the <u>brume</u> on this <u>paper</u>.
         E   F   G

                                NONE
8. Ⓔ   Ⓕ   Ⓖ   Ⓗ

9. She <u>kept</u> the <u>black</u> <u>glube</u> there.
       A   B   C

                                NONE
9. Ⓐ   Ⓑ   Ⓒ   Ⓓ

10. We <u>myght</u> have a new <u>excuse</u> from the <u>parade</u>.
        E   F   G

                              NONE
10. Ⓔ   Ⓕ   Ⓖ   Ⓗ

McGraw-Hill School Division

11. The <u>theef</u> was <u>thrown</u> from the <u>bicycle</u>.
      A   B   C

NONE
11. Ⓐ Ⓑ Ⓒ Ⓓ

12. This <u>thinng</u> was <u>kept</u> for the <u>season</u>.
     E   F   G

NONE
12. Ⓔ Ⓕ Ⓖ Ⓗ

13. Did you have <u>juice</u> with <u>toast</u> and <u>soop</u>?
            A   B   C

NONE
13. Ⓐ Ⓑ Ⓒ Ⓓ

14. I will <u>record</u> the <u>strike</u> on <u>paper</u>.
       E   F   G

NONE
14. Ⓔ Ⓕ Ⓖ Ⓗ

15. Dad makes <u>toste</u> and <u>juice</u> after we are <u>awake</u>.
          A   B   C

NONE
15. Ⓐ Ⓑ Ⓒ Ⓓ

16. She <u>kept</u> a <u>record</u> of the <u>ekscuse</u>.
     E   F   G

NONE
16. Ⓔ Ⓕ Ⓖ Ⓗ

17. When he is <u>awayk</u> he <u>might</u> have <u>juice</u>.
          A   B   C

NONE
17. Ⓐ Ⓑ Ⓒ Ⓓ

18. We <u>might</u> have a <u>parade</u> this <u>seezon</u>.
    E   F   G

NONE
18. Ⓔ Ⓕ Ⓖ Ⓗ

19. The <u>black</u> <u>rocks</u> were <u>throne</u> in the field.
     A   B   C

NONE
19. Ⓐ Ⓑ Ⓒ Ⓓ

20. We <u>kept</u> <u>joos</u> with <u>soup</u> in the kitchen.
     E F   G

NONE
20. Ⓔ Ⓕ Ⓖ Ⓗ

21. The <u>parade</u> made a new <u>reckord</u> <u>strike</u>.
     A   B   C

NONE
21. Ⓐ Ⓑ Ⓒ Ⓓ

22. The player <u>might</u> <u>strycke</u> out this <u>season</u>.
          E   F   G

NONE
22. Ⓔ Ⓕ Ⓖ Ⓗ

23. The <u>breeze</u> <u>might</u> help <u>lyfe</u> in the sea.
     A   B   C

NONE
23. Ⓐ Ⓑ Ⓒ Ⓓ

24. We <u>keptt</u> the <u>broom</u> in the blue <u>cage</u>.
     E   F   G

NONE
24. Ⓔ Ⓕ Ⓖ Ⓗ

25. That <u>paper</u> was new a <u>season</u> <u>ago</u>.
     A   B   C

NONE
25. Ⓐ Ⓑ Ⓒ Ⓓ

Syllable Patterns

Pretest Directions

Fold back the paper along the dotted line. Use the blanks to write each word as it is read aloud. When you finish the test, unfold the paper. Use the list at the right to correct any spelling mistakes. Practice the words you missed for the Posttest.

To Parents

Here are the results of your child's weekly spelling Pretest. You can help your child study for the Posttest by following these simple steps for each word on the word list:

1. Read the word to your child.
2. Have your child write the word, saying each letter as it is written.
3. Say each letter of the word as your child checks the spelling.
4. If a mistake has been made, have your child read each letter of the correctly spelled word aloud, and then repeat steps 1-3.

Parent/Child Activity:

Play a rhyming game with your child by taking turns saying as many rhyming words as you both can think of for each spelling word.

1. _____ 1. open
2. _____ 2. battle
3. _____ 3. even
4. _____ 4. candle
5. _____ 5. frozen
6. _____ 6. carrots
7. _____ 7. silent
8. _____ 8. bottle
9. _____ 9. lazy
10. _____ 10. lettuce
11. _____ 11. maple
12. _____ 12. fellow
13. _____ 13. fifty
14. _____ 14. flavor
15. _____ 15. floppy

Challenge Words

_____ area
_____ excitement
_____ halfway
_____ heap
_____ schedule

Syllable Patterns

Using the Word Study Steps

1. LOOK at the word.

2. SAY the word aloud.

3. STUDY the letters in the word.

4. WRITE the word.

5. CHECK the word.
   Did you spell the word right?
   If not, go back to step 1.

Spelling Tip

If a 2-syllable word has a short vowel sound in the first syllable, it is often followed by a two consonants or a double consonant.

Word Scramble

Unscramble each set of letters to make a spelling word.

1. npoe _____

2. yalz _____

3. ettabl _____

4. cuetetl _____

5. veen _____

6. pleam _____

7. elacnd _____

8. welofl _____

9. nrzoef _____

10. ytffi _____

11. roratcs _____

12. foravl _____

13. telnis _____

14. pyplfo _____

15. lettbo _____

To Parents or Helpers:
    Using the Word Study Steps above as your child comes across any new words will help him or her spell well. Review the steps as you both go over this week's spelling words.
    Go over the Spelling Tip with your child. Ask if he or she knows other 2-syllable words with a short vowel sound in the first syllable followed by two consonants or a double consonant.
    Help your child unscramble the spelling words in the puzzle.

Syllable Patterns

open	candle	silent	lettuce	fifty
battle	frozen	bottle	maple	flavor
even	carrots	lazy	fellow	floppy

Syllable Practice

Write the spelling words that contain a long-vowel sound in the first syllable.

1. _____ 2. _____ 3. _____

4. _____ 5. _____ 6. _____

7. _____

Write the spelling words that contain a short-vowel sound in the first syllable.

8. _____ 9. _____ 10. _____

11. _____ 12. _____ 13. _____

14. _____ 15. _____

Pattern Power!

Write the spelling words with each of these patterns.

fl

16. _____

17. _____

18. _____

fl

21. _____

22. _____

23. _____

24. _____

en

19. _____

20. _____

en

25. _____

26. _____

27. _____

Syllable Patterns

open	candle	silent	lettuce	fifty
battle	frozen	bottle	maple	flavor
even	carrots	lazy	fellow	floppy

A Fine Definition

Fill in the word from your spelling list that matches the definition.

1. Cooled to a very low temperature _____

2. A number written as 50 _____

3. Not willing to work _____

4. Making no sound _____

5. A leafy, green plant, eaten as salad _____

6. A fight between two armies _____

7. A taste of something _____

8. Vegetables with long yellow-orange roots _____

9. Not closed _____

10. A glass container _____

Word Journal

Copy six words from "A Fine Definition" onto a separate piece of paper. Look at the meanings again. Then write a sentence using each word.

Challenge Extension: Have students write a synonym for each Challenge Word, and then use that word in a sentence.

36

Book 3.1/Unit 2
City Green 16

McGraw-Hill School Division

Syllable Patterns

Proofreading Activity

There are six spelling mistakes in this paragraph. Circle the misspelled words. Write the words correctly on the lines below.

It was a laysy, sunny day. The gate by the garden was opun. Jean Marie saw a rabbit with flopee ears hop away. The girl knew there was trouble, because she and the rabbit were having an ongoing battel all summer long. She quickly checked her plants. Jean Marie found three were missing. All the leaves of the lettus plants were chewed. Then she spotted a bottul on the ground. Some mapil syrup had spilled from it. "There's nothing this rabbit won't eat!" she thought to herself.

1. _____ 2. _____ 3. _____

4. _____ 5. _____ 6. _____

Writing Activity

Write a description of a vegetable garden. Use at least three list words in your description.

_____

_____

_____

_____

Syllable Patterns

Look at the words in each set. One word in each set is spelled correctly.
Use a pencil to color in the circle in front of that word. Before you begin,
look at the sample sets of words. Sample A has been done for you.
Do Sample B by yourself. When you are sure you know what to do,
you may go on with the rest of the page.

Sample A
- Ⓐ aipron
- Ⓑ aprone
- ⓒ apron
- Ⓓ appron

Sample B
- Ⓔ settle
- Ⓕ setle
- Ⓖ cettle
- Ⓗ settal

1.
- Ⓐ carrots
- Ⓑ karots
- ⓒ karrots
- Ⓓ carits

2.
- Ⓔ mapul
- Ⓕ maple
- Ⓖ mayple
- Ⓗ mapel

3.
- Ⓐ flayver
- Ⓑ flavor
- ⓒ flavore
- Ⓓ flaiver

4.
- Ⓔ evin
- Ⓕ evon
- Ⓖ evun
- Ⓗ even

5.
- Ⓐ felow
- Ⓑ felloe
- ⓒ fellow
- Ⓓ felluh

6.
- Ⓔ open
- Ⓕ owpen
- Ⓖ opun
- Ⓗ oppen

7.
- Ⓐ battul
- Ⓑ batle
- ⓒ battle
- Ⓓ batel

8.
- Ⓔ silent
- Ⓕ sylent
- Ⓖ silen
- Ⓗ silunt

9.
- Ⓐ lettuse
- Ⓑ letuce
- ⓒ lettuce
- Ⓓ lettace

10.
- Ⓔ flopy
- Ⓕ flopee
- Ⓖ floppy
- Ⓗ floppey

11.
- Ⓐ layzee
- Ⓑ lazy
- ⓒ lazey
- Ⓓ lasy

12.
- Ⓔ candel
- Ⓕ kandle
- Ⓖ candul
- Ⓗ candle

13.
- Ⓐ botle
- Ⓑ botlle
- ⓒ bottal
- Ⓓ bottle

14.
- Ⓔ fiffty
- Ⓕ phifty
- Ⓖ fifty
- Ⓗ fiftee

15.
- Ⓐ frozen
- Ⓑ frowzen
- ⓒ frosen
- Ⓓ frozin

McGraw-Hill School Division

Words with Consonant Clusters

Pretest Directions

Fold back the paper along the dotted line. Use the blanks to write each word as it is read aloud. When you finish the test, unfold the paper. Use the list at the right to correct any spelling mistakes. Practice the words you missed for the Posttest.

To Parents

Here are the results of your child's weekly spelling Pretest. You can help your child study for the Posttest by following these simple steps for each word on the word list:

1. Read the word to your child.

2. Have your child write the word, saying each letter as it is written.

3. Say each letter of the word as your child checks the spelling.

4. If a mistake has been made, have your child read each letter of the correctly spelled word aloud, and then repeat steps 1-3.

1. _____ 1. block
2. _____ 2. brake
3. _____ 3. crazy
4. _____ 4. flash
5. _____ 5. grab
6. _____ 6. plate
7. _____ 7. blink
8. _____ 8. broad
9. _____ 9. crumble
10. _____ 10. flood
11. _____ 11. grand
12. _____ 12. blind
13. _____ 13. brisk
14. _____ 14. flame
15. _____ 15. plenty

Challenge Words

_____ canyons
_____ flowed
_____ grains
_____ handful
_____ peaks

McGraw-Hill School Division

Words with Consonant Clusters

Using the Word Study Steps

1. LOOK at the word.

2. SAY the word aloud.

3. STUDY the letters in the word.

4. WRITE the word.

5. CHECK the word.
   Did you spell the word right?
   If not, go back to step 1.

Spelling Tip

Use words that you know how to spell to help you spell new words:

black + r**ock** = **block**

Make Complete words

Use the letters in the boxes to begin words.

Circle the word endings that will correctly form spelling words.

bl		br		cr		fl		gr		pl	
ock	ink	ake	isk	azy	ode	isk	ame	ash	ick	ame	enty
isk	ash	ish	ock	ope	ame	ink	ash	osh	and	ock	ate
	ind		oad	umble		ood			ab		ind

To Parents or Helpers:

Using the Word Study Steps above as your child comes across any new words will help him or her spell well. Review the steps as you both go over this week's spelling words.

Go over the Spelling Tip with your child. Ask your child to think of other words he or she knows how to spell. Help him or her spell new words with the help of other words your child already knows.

Help your child find and circle the spelling words in the puzzle.

Words with Consonant Clusters

block	flash	blink	flood	brisk
brake	grab	broad	grand	flame
crazy	plate	crumble	blind	plenty

Pattern Power!

Write the spelling words that have these spelling patterns.

bl   **br**   **cr**

1. _____   4. _____   7. _____

2. _____   5. _____   8. _____

3. _____   6. _____

fl   **gr**   **pl**

9. _____   12. _____   14. _____

10. _____   13. _____

11. _____

Words Within Words

Write the spelling word that contains the small word.

15. risk _____   **16.** and _____

17. lock _____   **18.** ate _____

19. ash _____   **20.** ink _____

21. rake _____   **22.** road _____

Words with Consonant Clusters

block	flash	blink	flood	brisk
brake	grab	broad	grand	flame
crazy	plate	crumble	blind	plenty

Fill in the Blanks

Complete each sentence with a word from the spelling list.

1. I washed the _____ in the sink.

2. Because of the _____, the basement had two feet of water.

3. The driver pulled the emergency _____ to stop the train.

4. A crispy cookie will _____ into tiny bits.

5. The _____ from the oil lamp glowed yellow and red.

6. The prince and princess had a _____ time at the ball.

7. Watch the thief _____ the wallet and run!

8. In total darkness, a person is _____.

9. Did the prisoner have a sound mind or was he _____?

10. The _____ of lightning was followed by thunder.

"B" Matches

Write a spelling word that begins with the letter b to match each word clue.

11. moving quickly   _____

12. wide   _____

13. stop   _____

14. without the sense of sight _____

15. a quick wink of an eye   _____

Challenge Extension: Write the Challenge Words
on the board in scrambled order and ask
42 students to write them in ABC order.

Book 3.1/Unit 2
The Sun, the Wind, and the Rain 15

McGraw-Hill School Division

Words with Consonant Clusters

Proofreading Activity

There are 10 spelling mistakes in these directions. Circle the misspelled words. Write the words correctly on the lines below.

If you plan to travel by foot:

1. Go one blauk west.

2. Walk at a brissk pace.

3. Then skip across the brawd avenue.

4. Never mind, grabb a taxi instead!

If you plan to travel by car:

5. Slam on the emergency brak when you reach the driveway.

6. Then flasch your headlights three times.

1. _____ 2. _____ 3. _____

4. _____ 5. _____ 6. _____

Writing Activity

Write a set of directions telling how to get to a certain place. You could explain, for example, how to get to your school or to your nearest library. Number each step. Use several list words.

_____

_____

_____

_____

Words with Consonant Clusters

Look at the words in each set. One word in each set is spelled correctly.
Use a pencil to color in the circle in front of that word. Before you begin,
look at the sample sets of words. Sample A has been done for you.
Do Sample B by yourself. When you are sure you know what to do,
you may go on with the rest of the page.

Sample A
- (A) truk
- (B) truck
- (C) truak
- (D) druck

Sample B
- (E) blaime
- (F) blamme
- (G) blame
- (H) blaym

1.
- (A) flash
- (B) flashh
- (C) flasch
- (D) flach

6.
- (E) plate
- (F) playte
- (G) plaite
- (H) plait

11.
- (A) grabbe
- (B) grab
- (C) grabb
- (D) grabe

2.
- (E) crumble
- (F) crumbel
- (G) krumble
- (H) crummble

7.
- (A) blynk
- (B) blenk
- (C) blink
- (D) blienk

12.
- (E) plentie
- (F) plennty
- (G) plenty
- (H) plenity

3.
- (A) flud
- (B) fludd
- (C) flod
- (D) flood

8.
- (E) crazee
- (F) crazy
- (G) crazie
- (H) krazy

13.
- (A) granned
- (B) gran
- (C) grande
- (D) grand

4.
- (E) brissk
- (F) brisk
- (G) brysk
- (H) brisck

9.
- (A) blind
- (B) bliand
- (C) blinde
- (D) blynd

14.
- (E) brayk
- (F) brake
- (G) braik
- (H) braick

5.
- (A) broad
- (B) brawd
- (C) browd
- (D) brad

10.
- (E) flayme
- (F) flaim
- (G) flame
- (H) flaym

15.
- (A) blauk
- (B) block
- (C) blawk
- (D) blok

McGraw-Hill School Division

Pretest Directions

Fold back the paper along the dotted line. Use the blanks to write each word as it is read aloud. When you finish the test, unfold the paper. Use the list at the right to correct any spelling mistakes. Practice the words you missed for the Posttest.

To Parents

Here are the results of your child's weekly spelling Pretest. You can help your child study for the Posttest by following these simple steps for each word on the word list:

1. Read the word to your child.

2. Have your child write the word, saying each letter as it is written.

3. Say each letter of the word as your child checks the spelling.

4. If a mistake has been made, have your child read each letter of the correctly spelled word aloud, and then repeat steps 1-3.

1. _____ 1. spend

2. _____ 2. stream

3. _____ 3. scream

4. _____ 4. spring

5. _____ 5. skate

6. _____ 6. slept

7. _____ 7. spider

8. _____ 8. strong

9. _____ 9. scrub

10. _____ 10. sprinkle

11. _____ 11. skin

12. _____ 12. sleeve

13. _____ 13. string

14. _____ 14. screen

15. _____ 15. slice

Challenge Words

_____ buffalo

_____ darkness

_____ echoes

_____ ripe

_____ shelter

Words with Consonant Clusters

Using the Word Study Steps

1. LOOK at the word.

2. SAY the word aloud.

3. STUDY the letters in the word.

4. WRITE the word.

5. CHECK the word.
   Did you spell the word right?
   If not, go back to step 1.

Spelling Tip

Become familiar with the dictionary and use it often.

Find and Circle

Where are the spelling words?

```
s t r e a m x s p r i n k l e s s x
p s c r e a m k s l e e v e x l c s
e s p r i n g a s t r i n g y e r k
n s p i d e r t s c r e e n p p u i
d s t r o n g e x s l i c e z t b n
```

To Parents or Helpers:
   Using the Word Study Steps above as your child comes across any new words will help him or her spell well. Review the steps as you both go over this week's spelling words.
   Go over the Spelling Tip with your child. Help your child learn to use the dictionary when he or she needs help with a word.
   Help your child find and circle the spelling words in the puzzle.

McGraw-Hill School Division

Words with Consonant Clusters

spend	spring	spider	sprinkle	string
stream	skate	strong	skin	screen
scream	slept	scrub	sleeve	slice

Fill in the Blanks

Complete the sentences with list words that have the same spelling pattern. You may use some words more than once.

sp

1. I never _____ my whole allowance.
2. The _____ crawled onto his foot.

sk

3. Don't _____ on thin ice.
4. The sun and wind make my _____ dry.

sl

5. It was so noisy I hardly _____.
6. The _____ on my shirt was too short.
7. I'll have another _____ of pie.

str

8. The _____ made a bubbly sound.
9. He's _____ enough to lift anything.
10. The balloon is only held by a _____.

scr

11. The sudden sound made me _____.
12. We saw the movie on a very big _____.
13. If you _____ hard you can clean it.

spr

14. In the _____ the snow melted.
15. A light _____ of rain made the flower bloom.

Rhyme Time

Write the spelling words that rhyme with the words below.

16. cream _____ _____

17. swing _____ _____

18. twice _____

19. state _____

20. stub _____

Words with Consonant Clusters

spend	spring	spider	sprinkle	string
stream	skate	strong	skin	screen
scream	slept	scrub	sleeve	slice

Words in Sentences

Read each clue across and down. Use spelling words to complete this puzzle.

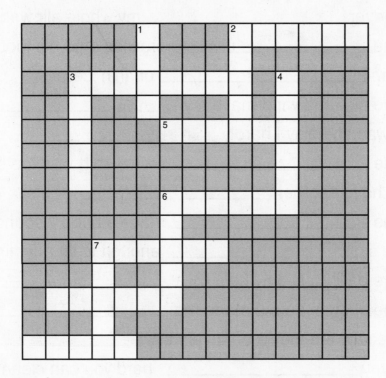

ACROSS

2. It lets the air in but keeps the bugs out
3. Put nuts on a sundae
5. Web spinner
6. After winter
7. One of lots on a harp
8. The part of a shirt that covers the arm
9. You can do it on ice or inline

DOWN

1. It's all over you
2. The opposite of save
3. Rub until clean
4. Pie section
7. Took a nap

Challenge Extension: Have students create a word-search puzzle using all Challenge Words and exchange papers with a partner to solve it.

Book 3.1/Unit 2
Dream Wolf
13

McGraw-Hill School Division

Words with Consonant Clusters

Proofreading Activity

There are 6 spelling mistakes in this paragraph. Circle the misspelled words. Write the words correctly on the lines below.

Spring is a great time of year for Roger. He likes to spen time at the park. The trees have turned green with new leaves. Plants have started to bloom. Roger can scate along a special trail that takes him by the water. The streem looks inviting, but Roger knows it's too dangerous to play there. He'll just sprinckal some water on his face. The water feels too cool on his scin, and Roger wipes his face on his sleve. Maybe later Roger will fly his kite.

1. _____ 2. _____ 3. _____

4. _____ 5. _____ 6. _____

Writing Activity

What season of the year do you like best? Write about it. Explain what you like most about you favorite season. Use four words from your spelling list. Circle any words you use that have consonant clusters.

_____

_____

_____

_____

Words with Consonant Clusters

Look at the words in each set. One word in each set is spelled correctly.
Use a pencil to color in the circle in front of that word. Before you begin,
look at the sample sets of words. Sample A has been done for you.
Do Sample B by yourself. When you are sure you know what to do,
you may go on with the rest of the page.

Sample A
- Ⓐ steet
- Ⓑ srete
- Ⓒ streat
- ● street

Sample B
- Ⓔ skrap
- Ⓕ scrap
- Ⓖ scrapp
- Ⓗ scarp

1.
- Ⓐ scrubb
- Ⓑ scub
- Ⓒ scrub
- Ⓓ scroub

2.
- Ⓔ sleave
- Ⓕ sleeve
- Ⓖ sleve
- Ⓗ sleev

3.
- Ⓐ salice
- Ⓑ slice
- Ⓒ slise
- Ⓓ clice

4.
- Ⓔ stream
- Ⓕ sream
- Ⓖ streem
- Ⓗ streme

5.
- Ⓐ scate
- Ⓑ skait
- Ⓒ scayt
- Ⓓ skate

6.
- Ⓔ strong
- Ⓕ stong
- Ⓖ stron
- Ⓗ strawng

7.
- Ⓐ spund
- Ⓑ speand
- Ⓒ spend
- Ⓓ spende

8.
- Ⓔ sprring
- Ⓕ spring
- Ⓖ springe
- Ⓗ sprig

9.
- Ⓐ scin
- Ⓑ skine
- Ⓒ skin
- Ⓓ skinn

10.
- Ⓔ screen
- Ⓕ skreen
- Ⓖ screan
- Ⓗ scaren

11.
- Ⓐ stering
- Ⓑ string
- Ⓒ strin
- Ⓓ strink

12.
- Ⓔ spida
- Ⓕ spidor
- Ⓖ spidder
- Ⓗ spider

13.
- Ⓐ skream
- Ⓑ screem
- Ⓒ scareme
- Ⓓ scream

14.
- Ⓔ slept
- Ⓕ sleped
- Ⓖ salept
- Ⓗ slepd

15.
- Ⓐ sprincle
- Ⓑ sprinkle
- Ⓒ spinkle
- Ⓓ spinkal

Plurals

Pretest Directions

Fold back the paper along the dotted line. Use the blanks to write each word as it is read aloud. When you finish the test, unfold the paper. Use the list at the right to correct any spelling mistakes. Practice the words you missed for the Posttest.

To Parents

Here are the results of your child's weekly spelling Pretest. You can help your child study for the Posttest by following these simple steps for each word on the word list:

1. Read the word to your child.

2. Have your child write the word, saying each letter as it is written.

3. Say each letter of the word as your child checks the spelling.

4. If a mistake has been made, have your child read each letter of the correctly spelled word aloud, and then repeat steps 1-3.

#		#	Word
1.	_____	1.	blankets
2.	_____	2.	branches
3.	_____	3.	flies
4.	_____	4.	mountains
5.	_____	5.	states
6.	_____	6.	libraries
7.	_____	7.	pairs
8.	_____	8.	bunches
9.	_____	9.	enemies
10.	_____	10.	pockets
11.	_____	11.	jungles
12.	_____	12.	daisies
13.	_____	13.	inches
14.	_____	14.	companies
15.	_____	15.	addresses

Challenge Words

_____ capture

_____ liquid

_____ ruin

_____ skills

_____ struggles

McGraw-Hill School Division

Plurals

Using the Word Study Steps

1. LOOK at the word.

2. SAY the word aloud.

3. STUDY the letters in the word.

4. WRITE the word.

5. CHECK the word.
   Did you spell the word right?
   If not, go back to step 1.

Spelling Tip
Add **-s** to most words to form plurals or to change the tense of verbs. Add **-es** to words ending in **x**, **z**, **s**, **sh**, or **ch**.
pair + s = pairs
buzz + es = buzzes
When a word ends with a consonant followed by **y**, change the **y** to **i** and add **-es**.
library + es = libraries

X the Words

Put an X on the word that does not fit the spelling pattern.

1.	pairs	pockets	inch	bunches
2.	flies	enemy	daisies	libraries
3.	company	blankets	state	jungle
4.	mountain	addresses	branches	pairs
5.	jungles	mountains	addresses	company
6.	fly	blankets	libraries	enemies
7.	pocket	inch	jungles	library
8.	addresses	bunches	pair	branches
9.	companies	states	mountains	enemy
10.	daisy	jungle	branches	fly

To Parents or Helpers:

Using the Word Study Steps above as your child comes across any new words will help him or her spell well. Review the steps as you both go over this week's spelling words.

Go over each Spelling Tip with your child. Ask him or her to add **-s** or **-es** to other words to form plurals. Ask if he or she knows other words that end with a consonant followed by **y**. Help him or her add endings to the words, using the rule.

Help your child find and cross out the word that doesn't fit the spelling pattern in the puzzle.

Book 3.1/Unit 2
Spiders at Work 10

McGraw-Hill School Division

Plurals

blankets	mountains	pairs	pockets	inches
branches	states	bunches	jungles	companies
flies	libraries	enemies	daisies	addresses

This week's spelling list contains plural words. **Plurals** are words that name more than one thing.

Write the spelling words for each of these plural endings.

s

1. _____
2. _____
3. _____
4. _____
5. _____
6. _____

y to i + es

11. _____
12. _____
13. _____
14. _____
15. _____

es

7. _____
8. _____
9. _____
10. _____

Find the Base Word

Write the base word of each plural noun.

16. blankets _____   17. flies _____

18. libraries _____   19. branches_____

Plurals

blankets	mountains	pairs	pockets	inches
branches	states	bunches	jungles	companies
flies	libraries	enemies	daisies	addresses

Part of the Group

Add the spelling word that belongs in each group, below.

Flowers

1. roses, lilies, _____

Measurements

2. yards, feet, _____

Tree Parts

3. _____

Insects

4. ants, bugs, _____

Two of a Kind

5. twins, doubles, _____

Governments

6. countries, cities, _____

A Clue for You

Read each clue. Then write the list word that fits the clue.

7. These mean the opposite of friends. _____

8. They are taller than hills. _____

9. Bananas grow in these groups. So do grapes. _____

10. These are placed on top of sheets for warmth. _____

11. You'll find plenty of books in these places. _____

12. You can find spare change in these. _____

13. These are often hot and sticky places. _____

14. These are also called businesses. _____

15. Many people keep these in a little book. _____

Challenge Extension: Have students write a "fill in the blank word" for each Challenge Word, then work with a partner to complete each other's sentences.

54

Book 3.1/Unit 2 / 15
Spiders at Work

McGraw-Hill School Division

Plurals

Proofreading Activity

There are 6 spelling mistakes in this fact book outline. Circle the misspelled words. Write the words correctly on the lines below.

Facts About Hawaii

I.   Geography and climate

    A.   Mountins and volcanoes

    B.   Rain forests and jungeles

    C.   Natural enemes of weather

    D.   Average rainfall measured in inchez

II.   Government and Education

    A.   Branches of government

    B.   Schools and special libarees

III.   Other State Facts

    A.   Transportation and Tourism

    B.   State symbols

    C.   Top 10 companyes

1. _____   2. _____   3. _____

4. _____   5. _____   6. _____

Writing Activity

Use four spelling words. Describe an insect or bird that most expresses to you the beauty of flying. Write about how it looks and acts while it is in flight. Circle any plural words you use.

_____

_____

_____

_____

Plurals

Look at the words in each set. One word in each set is spelled correctly.
Use a pencil to color in the circle in front of that word. Before you begin,
look at the sample sets of words. Sample A has been done for you.
Do Sample B by yourself. When you are sure you know what to do,
you may go on with the rest of the page.

Sample A
Ⓐ pinches
Ⓑ pinchs
Ⓒ pintches
Ⓓ pinchis

Sample B
Ⓔ heries
Ⓕ huries
Ⓖ hurrys
Ⓗ hurries

1. Ⓐ flies
   Ⓑ flize
   Ⓒ fleise
   Ⓓ flys

6. Ⓔ inchez
   Ⓕ inchs
   Ⓖ intches
   Ⓗ inches

11. Ⓐ bunchez
    Ⓑ bunchuz
    Ⓒ buntches
    Ⓓ bunches

2. Ⓔ pocketes
   Ⓕ pockets
   Ⓖ pocketts
   Ⓗ poketts

7. Ⓐ montains
   Ⓑ mountaines
   Ⓒ mountains
   Ⓓ mountens

12. Ⓔ librarys
    Ⓕ libraries
    Ⓖ librairies
    Ⓗ liberaries

3. Ⓐ blanckets
   Ⓑ blanquetts
   Ⓒ blankets
   Ⓓ blankits

8. Ⓔ daisies
   Ⓕ daysies
   Ⓖ dazies
   Ⓗ dasies

13. Ⓐ staits
    Ⓑ states
    Ⓒ staights
    Ⓓ staites

4. Ⓔ jungles
   Ⓕ jungleses
   Ⓖ junguls
   Ⓗ jungels

9. Ⓐ companys
   Ⓑ compnies
   Ⓒ commpanies
   Ⓓ companies

14. Ⓔ addreses
    Ⓕ adresses
    Ⓖ addresses
    Ⓗ adrusses

5. Ⓐ paires
   Ⓑ pairs
   Ⓒ pars
   Ⓓ peirs

10. Ⓔ enemies
    Ⓕ enemys
    Ⓖ enemmies
    Ⓗ enumies

Words from Science

Pretest Directions

Fold back the paper along the dotted line. Use the blanks to write each word as it is read aloud. When you finish the test, unfold the paper. Use the list at the right to correct any spelling mistakes. Practice the words you missed for the Posttest.

To Parents

Here are the results of your child's weekly spelling Pretest. You can help your child study for the Posttest by following these simple steps for each word on the word list:

1. Read the word to your child.

2. Have your child write the word, saying each letter as it is written.

3. Say each letter of the word as your child checks the spelling.

4. If a mistake has been made, have your child read each letter of the correctly spelled word aloud, and then repeat steps 1-3.

1. _____ 1. web

2. _____ 2. sticky

3. _____ 3. bait

4. _____ 4. cell

5. _____ 5. silk

6. _____ 6. weave

7. _____ 7. fiber

8. _____ 8. strands

9. _____ 9. beetle

10. _____ 10. thread

11. _____ 11. science

12. _____ 12. fang

13. _____ 13. breathe

14. _____ 14. taste

15. _____ 15. prey

Challenge Words

_____ XXXXXX

_____ XXXXXX

_____ XXXXXX

_____ XXXXXX

_____ XXXXXX

Words from Science

Using the Word Study Steps

1. LOOK at the word.

2. SAY the word aloud.

3. STUDY the letters in the word.

4. WRITE the word.

5. CHECK the word.
   Did you spell the word right?
   If not, go back to step 1.

Spelling Tip

When the **/s/** sound is spelled **c**, **c** is always followed by **e**, **i**, or **y**.

Example:
    cells

Think of a related word to help you spell a word with a silent letter or a hard-to-hear sound.

Example:
    breath   breathe

Word Scramble

Unscramble each set of letters to make a spelling word.

1. bew _____   **2.** tiab _____   **3.** trssdna _____

4. yerp _____   **5.** gnaf _____   **6.** ksli _____

7. rfbei _____   **8.** ettsa _____   **9.** hretabe _____

10. ystcyik _____   **11.** lbteee _____   **12.** vaewe _____

13. llce _____   **14.** dretah _____   **15.** nseicec _____

To Parents or Helpers:

Using the Word Study Steps above as your child comes across any new words will help him or her spell well. Review the steps as you both go over this week's spelling words.

Go over each Spelling Tip with your child. Ask him or her to write and study other words with the /s/ sound spelled c. Help your child think of other related words that help him or her spell a word with a silent letter or a hard-to-hear sound.

Help your child find and unscramble the spelling words in the puzzle.

McGraw-Hill School Division

Words from Science

web	cell	fiber	thread	breathe
sticky	silk	strands	science	taste
bait	weave	beetle	fang	prey

Pattern Power

Write the spelling words with short **e** .

1. _____   2. _____   3. _____

Write the spelling words with long **e**.

4. _____   5. _____   6. _____

Write the spelling words with long **i**.

7. _____   8. _____

Write the spelling words with short **i**.

9. _____   10. _____

Write the spelling words with long **a**.

11. _____   12. _____

13. _____

Write the spelling words with short **a**.

14. _____   15. _____

Words from Science

web	cell	fiber	thread	breathe
sticky	silk	strands	science	taste
bait	weave	beetle	fang	prey

It Takes Three
Write a spelling word that goes with the other two words.

1. cotton, wool, _____   **2.** gooey, icky, _____

3. net, trap, _____   **4.** bee, fly, _____

5. eat, munch, _____   **6.** cage, prison, _____

What Do You Mean?
Read each dictionary definition below. Then write the spelling word that matches the definition.

7. To form strands into a web   _____

8. The study and explanation of knowledge   _____

9. An animal that is hunted   _____

10. A long, pointed snake's tooth   _____

11. To take air into and out from the lungs   _____

12. Food placed on a hook or in a trap to
get animals   _____

Word Journal
Use the spelling words *fiber*, *strand* and *thread* each in a sentence.

13. _____

14. _____

15. _____

60

Challenge Extension: Have students write dictionary definitions of
the Challenge Words. Then exchange papers with a partner and
write the Challenge Word that matches each definition.

Book 3.1/Unit 2
Web Wonders 15

McGraw-Hill School Division

Words from Science

Proofreading Activity

There are 6 spelling mistakes in this poem. Circle the misspelled words. Write the words correctly on the lines below.

Web Nonsense

This spider's name is Nicky.
Its web is gooey and stickey.
Its strandes are smooth as silck
Or very rich buttermilk.
You may well not believe
How gently Nicky can weeve
Each fine thread into a net.
That's when the trap is set!
For every fibur is a way
To trap some poor insect preay.

1. _____ 2. _____ 3. _____

4. _____ 5. _____ 6. _____

Writing Activity

Write four words that rhyme with the spelling words. Then write a nonsense poem using pairs of rhyming words. Use Use the poem above as a model.

Words That Rhyme   **Your Nonsense Poem**

7. _____   _____

8. _____   _____

9. _____   _____

10. _____   _____

Words from Science

Look at the words in each set. One word in each set is spelled correctly.
Use a pencil to color in the circle in front of that word. Before you begin,
look at the sample sets of words. Sample A has been done for you.
Do Sample B by yourself. When you are sure you know what to do,
you may go on with the rest of the page.

Sample A
- (A) milck
- (B) milc
- (C) milk
- (D) millk

Sample B
- (E) paste
- (F) payst
- (G) paist
- (H) pased

1.
- (A) cilk
- (B) silke
- (C) sillk
- (D) silk

2.
- (E) srands
- (F) strandes
- (G) strands
- (H) strandz

3.
- (A) betle
- (B) beetle
- (C) beetel
- (D) beetl

4.
- (E) preay
- (F) preye
- (G) prey
- (H) pey

5.
- (A) web
- (B) webb
- (C) wheb
- (D) webe

6.
- (E) bait
- (F) bayt
- (G) bate
- (H) batte

7.
- (A) sticy
- (B) sticky
- (C) stiky
- (D) stickey

8.
- (E) weeve
- (F) weabe
- (G) weve
- (H) weave

9.
- (A) science
- (B) sciense
- (C) sience
- (D) cience

10.
- (E) kell
- (F) sel
- (G) cell
- (H) scell

11.
- (A) taste
- (B) tast
- (C) tase
- (D) taist

12.
- (E) fang
- (F) fange
- (G) phang
- (H) fangk

13.
- (A) breethe
- (B) breyh
- (C) brete
- (D) breathe

14.
- (E) thred
- (F) thread
- (G) thedd
- (H) thrad

15.
- (A) fibur
- (B) fiber
- (C) fyber
- (D) phibore

McGraw-Hill School Division

Book 3.1/Unit 2 Review Test

Read each sentence. If an underlined word is spelled wrong, fill in the circle that goes with that word. If no word is spelled wrong, fill in the circle below NONE. Read Sample A, and do Sample B.

A. Please <u>close</u> the <u>door</u> <u>again</u>.
       A   B   C

NONE
A. Ⓐ Ⓑ Ⓒ ●

B. The <u>breeze</u> <u>kept</u> me <u>awacke</u>.
      E   F   G

NONE
B. Ⓔ Ⓕ Ⓖ Ⓗ

1. Use the <u>brayke</u> to <u>skate</u> on the <u>open</u> road.
         A   B   C

NONE
1. Ⓐ Ⓑ Ⓒ Ⓓ

2. He had to <u>blink</u> when he <u>blew</u> out the <u>candel</u>.
          E   F   G

NONE
2. Ⓔ Ⓕ Ⓖ Ⓗ

3. I <u>ate</u> this <u>slice</u> of <u>littuce</u>.
   A   B   C

NONE
3. Ⓐ Ⓑ Ⓒ Ⓓ

4. Did you <u>know</u> that <u>silke</u> is not made by a <u>beetle</u>?
        E   F   G

NONE
4. Ⓔ Ⓕ Ⓖ Ⓗ

5. The <u>fellowe</u> likes to <u>spend</u> time in <u>libraries</u>.
      A   B   C

NONE
5. Ⓐ Ⓑ Ⓒ Ⓓ

6. The <u>playte</u> is full of <u>frozen</u> <u>lettuce</u>.
      E   F   G

NONE
6. Ⓔ Ⓕ Ⓖ Ⓗ

7. In <u>spring</u>, there was a <u>flood</u> in the <u>mountians</u>.
     A   B   C

NONE
7. Ⓐ Ⓑ Ⓒ Ⓓ

8. The <u>flies</u> are <u>inshes</u> away on the <u>branches</u>.
      E   F   G

NONE
8. Ⓔ Ⓕ Ⓖ Ⓗ

9. You cannot <u>taste</u> the <u>fibber</u> in <u>lettuce</u>.
         A   B   C

NONE
9. Ⓐ Ⓑ Ⓒ Ⓓ

10. The <u>snake</u> did not <u>taste</u> with his <u>fang</u>.
       E   F   G

NONE
10. Ⓔ Ⓕ Ⓖ Ⓗ

NONE

11. I need to <u>blinke</u> in a <u>strong</u> <u>wind</u>.
        A   B   C

11. Ⓐ Ⓑ Ⓒ Ⓓ

NONE

12. I won't <u>skayt</u> on the <u>frozen</u> <u>branches</u>.
           E   F   G

12. Ⓔ Ⓕ Ⓖ Ⓗ

NONE

13. She <u>flies</u> into the <u>mountains</u> in a <u>floode</u>.
      A   B   C

13. Ⓐ Ⓑ Ⓒ Ⓓ

NONE

14. The <u>betle</u> will <u>taste</u> that <u>plant</u>.
      E   F   G

14. Ⓔ Ⓕ Ⓖ Ⓗ

NONE

15. The <u>libraries</u> are <u>open</u> in the <u>springe</u>.
      A   B   C

15. Ⓐ Ⓑ Ⓒ Ⓓ

NONE

16. The <u>silk</u> worm <u>crawls</u> on the <u>branchis</u>.
     E   F   G

16. Ⓔ Ⓕ Ⓖ Ⓗ

NONE

17. I need to <u>brake</u> on the <u>frozin</u> <u>mountains</u>.
        A   B   C

17. Ⓐ Ⓑ Ⓒ Ⓓ

NONE

18. You can find <u>books</u> in <u>liberries</u> that are <u>open</u>.
             E   F   G

18. Ⓔ Ⓕ Ⓖ Ⓗ

NONE

19. The <u>fiber</u> rope is <u>stronge</u> and made of <u>silk</u>.
      A   B   C

19. Ⓐ Ⓑ Ⓒ Ⓓ

NONE

20. I do not like to <u>spende</u> the <u>spring</u> in a <u>flood</u>.
             E   F   G

20. Ⓔ Ⓕ Ⓖ Ⓗ

NONE

21. <u>Would</u> you like to <u>taste</u> a <u>slyse</u> of cake?
    A   B   C

21. Ⓐ Ⓑ Ⓒ Ⓓ

NONE

22. The <u>beetle</u> only <u>flys</u> <u>inches</u>.
      E   F G

22. Ⓔ Ⓕ Ⓖ Ⓗ

NONE

23. The <u>snake</u> had a <u>strong</u> <u>fayng</u>.
      A   B   C

23. Ⓐ Ⓑ Ⓒ Ⓓ

NONE

24. You can <u>crumbel</u> the <u>candle</u> on the <u>plate</u>.
        E   F   G

24. Ⓔ Ⓕ Ⓖ Ⓗ

NONE

25. Please <u>opin</u> the <u>window</u> only <u>inches</u>.
       A   B   C

25. Ⓐ Ⓑ Ⓒ Ⓓ

McGraw-Hill School Division

Words with Consonant Clusters

Pretest Directions

Fold back the paper along the dotted line. Use the blanks to write each word as it is read aloud. When you finish the test, unfold the paper. Use the list at the right to correct any spelling mistakes. Practice the words you missed for the Posttest.

To Parents

Here are the results of your child's weekly spelling Pretest. You can help your child study for the Posttest by following these simple steps for each word on the word list:

1. Read the word to your child.

2. Have your child write the word, saying each letter as it is written.

3. Say each letter of the word as your child checks the spelling.

4. If a mistake has been made, have your child read each letter of the correctly spelled word aloud, and then repeat steps 1-3.

1. _____	1. paint
2. _____	2. young
3. _____	3. stamp
4. _____	4. thank
5. _____	5. friend
6. _____	6. ink
7. _____	7. behind
8. _____	8. faint
9. _____	9. swing
10. _____	10. thump
11. _____	11. belong
12. _____	12. student
13. _____	13. husband
14. _____	14. parent
15. _____	15. trunk

Challenge Words

_____ concert

_____ conductor

_____ instrument

_____ musician

_____ orchestrad

McGraw-Hill School Division

Words with Consonant Clusters

Using the Word Study Steps

1. LOOK at the word.

2. SAY the word aloud.

3. STUDY the letters in the wor

4. WRITE the word.

5. CHECK the word.
   Did you spell the word right?
   If not, go back to step 1.

<table>
<tr><td>Spelling Tip

Use words that you know how to spell to help you spell new words.

thin + bank = thank</td></tr>
</table>

X the Word

Put an X on the word that does not match the pattern.

thank	ink	trunk	truck
stamp	thump	stop	bump
below	swing	belong	young
friend	husband	behind	hushed
paint	study	student	parent

To Parents or Helpers:
    Using the Word Study Steps above as your child comes across any new words will help him or her spell well. Review the steps as you both go over this week's spelling words.
    Go over the Spelling Tip with your child. Help him or her spell new words by using familiar words.
    Help your child cross out the words that do not match the pattern in each row.

Words with Consonant Clusters

paint	thank	behind	thump	husband
young	friend	faint	belong	parent
stamp	ink	swing	student	trunk

Pattern Power

Write the spelling words for each of these clusters below.

nk

1. _____

2. _____

3. _____

mp

4. _____

5. _____

ng

6. _____

7. _____

8. _____

nd

9. _____

10. _____

11. _____

nt

12. _____

13. _____

14. _____

15. _____

Guide Words

Dictionary guide words help you find your way. Which spelling words will you find between each pair of words?

than/thunder **16.** _____ **17.** _____

pail/part **18.** _____ **19.** _____

face/front **20.** _____ **21.** _____

Word Hunt

Write the spelling word in which you can find the smaller word.

22. *hum* _____ **23.** *end* _____

24. *win* _____ **25.** *rent* _____

26. *long* _____ **27.** *dent* _____

28. *band* _____

Words with Consonant Clusters

paint	thank	behind	thump	husband
young	friend	faint	belong	parent
stamp	ink	swing	student	trunk

Opposites

An antonym is a word that has the opposite meaning of another word. Write the spelling word that is the antonym of each of the following words.

1. old _____

2. enemy _____

3. ahead _____

4. wife _____

What's the Word?

Write a spelling word that correctly completes the sentence.

5. The _____ studies math in the third grade.

6. This _____ spoke to the principal about her son.

7. I will _____ a picture with watercolors.

8. A _____ is married to his wife.

9. He keeps his spare tire in the _____ of his car.

10. _____ your arms left and right to the music.

11. _____ is the opposite of enemy.

12. The person sitting in back of you is _____ you.

Make a Sentence

Use each word in a sentence.

13. thank _____

14. faint _____

15. thump _____

16. belong _____

Challenge Extension: Have students draw and label a picture to illustrate each Challenge Word.

Grade 3.1/Unit 3
Moses Goes to a Concert
16

McGraw-Hill School Division

Words with Consonant Clusters

Proofreading Paragraph

There are six spelling mistakes in this paragraph. Circle the misspelled words. Write the words correctly on the lines below.

"How do the artists draw their cartoons?" Lisa asked.

"Some people use black inck to outline their figures," Mr. Lopez said. "I know other artists who use paynt."

"Who writes the studnt pages in your newspaper?" the girl asked.

"The group is made up of reporters and yung volunteers," the editor answered. A parrunt is also part of this team."

"Can a frind and I join this group?" she asked.

"Well, you'll both have to take a writing test," he said.

1. _____   2. _____   3. _____

4. _____   5. _____   6. _____

Writing Activity

What questions would you like to ask someone who works on a newspaper? Write your interview questions, using at least four spelling words.

_____

_____

_____

_____

_____

_____

Words with Consonant Clusters

Look at the words in each set. One word in each set is spelled correctly.
Use a pencil to color in the circle in front of that word. Before you begin,
look at the sample sets of words. Sample A has been done for you.
Do Sample B by yourself. When you are sure you know what to do,
you may go on with the rest of the page.

Sample A
- Ⓐ tangk
- ⬤Ⓑ tank
- Ⓒ tanek
- Ⓓ tanc

Sample B
- Ⓔ thinge
- Ⓕ thig
- Ⓖ thign
- Ⓗ thing

1.
- Ⓐ youn
- Ⓑ yung
- Ⓒ young
- Ⓓ younk

2.
- Ⓔ ink
- Ⓕ ingk
- Ⓖ inck
- Ⓗ inke

3.
- Ⓐ studet
- Ⓑ student
- Ⓒ studen
- Ⓓ studend

4.
- Ⓔ pante
- Ⓕ paynt
- Ⓖ paink
- Ⓗ paint

5.
- Ⓐ belone
- Ⓑ belong
- Ⓒ belawng
- Ⓓ belon

6.
- Ⓔ behind
- Ⓕ bahind
- Ⓖ behined
- Ⓗ bihine

7.
- Ⓐ thak
- Ⓑ thangk
- Ⓒ thanc
- Ⓓ thank

8.
- Ⓔ swin
- Ⓕ swingk
- Ⓖ swing
- Ⓗ swinge

9.
- Ⓐ trunc
- Ⓑ trunk
- Ⓒ trunkk
- Ⓓ trungk

10.
- Ⓔ stamb
- Ⓕ stemp
- Ⓖ stamp
- Ⓗ stap

11.
- Ⓐ parunt
- Ⓑ parrent
- Ⓒ parind
- Ⓓ parent

12.
- Ⓔ husban
- Ⓕ husbend
- Ⓖ husband
- Ⓗ husbant

13.
- Ⓐ friend
- Ⓑ frend
- Ⓒ frened
- Ⓓ fren

14.
- Ⓔ thumbp
- Ⓕ thump
- Ⓖ thup
- Ⓗ tump

15.
- Ⓐ faynt
- Ⓑ fanet
- Ⓒ faint
- Ⓓ faind

McGraw-Hill School Division

Words with Double Consonants

Pretest Directions

Fold back the paper along the dotted line. Use the blanks to write each word as it is read aloud. When you finish the test, unfold the paper. Use the list at the right to correct any spelling mistakes. Practice the words you missed for the Posttest.

To Parents

Here are the results of your child's weekly spelling Pretest. You can help your child study for the Posttest by following these simple steps for each word on the word list:

1. Read the word to your child.

2. Have your child write the word, saying each letter as it is written.

3. Say each letter of the word as your child checks the spelling.

4. If a mistake has been made, have your child read each letter of the correctly spelled word aloud, and then repeat steps 1-3.

1. _____	1. small
2. _____	2. ladder
3. _____	3. little
4. _____	4. happen
5. _____	5. rubber
6. _____	6. grass
7. _____	7. ribbon
8. _____	8. lesson
9. _____	9. silly
10. _____	10. butter
11. _____	11. supper
12. _____	12. middle
13. _____	13. possible
14. _____	14. hobby
15. _____	15. unhappy

Challenge Words

_____	blossoms
_____	dawn
_____	imaginary
_____	miserable
_____	shallow

McGraw-Hill School Division

Words with Double Consonants

Using the Word Study Steps

1. LOOK at the word.

2. SAY the word aloud.

3. STUDY the letters in the wor

4. WRITE the word.

5. CHECK the word.
   Did you spell the word right?
   If not, go back to step 1.

Spelling Tip

If you hear a short vowel sound followed by one consonant sound, it is often a double consonant. See if the spelling looks right with a double consonant. Use your dictionary if you are not sure.

Find and Circle

Where are the spelling words?

```
m i d d l e t l a d d e r u l i t t l e
u n h a p p y v s u p p e r x s i l l y
q s m a l l u l e s s o n o r i b b o n
p o s s i b l e n g r a s s h h o b b y
a b u t t e r x r u b b e r h a p p e n
```

To Parents or Helpers:
Using the Word Study Steps above as your child comes across any new words will help him or her spell well. Review the steps as you both go over this week's spelling words.
Go over the Spelling Tip with your child. Point out how each spelling word follows this pattern. Help your child use the dictionary to look up words. Help your child find and circle the spelling words in the puzzle.

McGraw-Hill School Division

Words with Double Consonants

small	happen	ribbon	butter	possible
ladder	rubber	lesson	supper	hobby
little	grass	silly	middle	unhappy

Pattern Power

Write the spelling words that have these spelling patterns.

tt

1. _____

2. _____

bb

5. _____

6. _____

7. _____

pp

10. _____

11. _____

12. _____

ll

3. _____

4. _____

dd

8. _____

9. _____

ss

13. _____

14. _____

15. _____

Rhyme Time

Write the spelling word that rhymes with each word.

16. rod _____

18. light _____

20. rod _____

22. rod _____

24. light _____

17. go _____

19. row _____

21. go _____

23. go _____

Words with Double Consonants

small	happen	ribbon	butter	possible
ladder	rubber	lesson	supper	hobby
little	grass	silly	middle	unhappy

Words in Sentences

Decide which spelling word fits in each sentence. Fill in the missing letters.

1. This sweater comes in sma____, medium, and large sizes.

2. Another word for small is li____le.

3. The medium-sized sweaters are in the mi____le of the counter.

4. Jonathan bought a green shirt that was the color of gra____.

5. What will ha____en if you wash it in hot water?

6. Yolanda chose a yellow dress like the color of bu____er.

7. She also wore a yellow ri____on in her hair.

8. Nicholas spilled gravy on his new suit during su____er.

9. It wasn't po____ible to wash the stain out.

10. The boy was so unha____y, he couldn't eat!

11. He learned a hard le____on because he wasn't careful.

Word Journal

One of the spelling words is hobby. Do you have a hobby, or a favorite pastime? Write a short description about what you like to work at or collect. Use four spelling words in your description.

_____

_____

McGraw-Hill School Division

Challenge Extension: Write the Challenge Words on the board in scrambled letter order and ask students to unscramble and write them correctly.

Grade 3.1/Unit 3
The Little Painter of Sabana Grande

15

Words with Double Consonants

Proofreading Paragraph

There are six spelling mistakes in this report. Circle the misspelled words. Write the words correctly on the lines below.

My Visit to America

I noticed many differences between American things and Japanese things. Some of them seem silly, but I'll include them, anyway. The gras looks greener in Vermont than in Tokyo. However, the buter tastes sweeter in my home country. I eat supperr earlier at home.

At first, I felt unhapy in a new country. How strange everything was! Then my American friend showed me his baseball card collection. When I helped him with his hoby, I was no longer sad. I learned an important lesson from my trip. If you don't want to be homesick, keep busy.

1. _____   2. _____   3. _____

4. _____   5. _____   6. _____

Writing Activity

Imagine that you are a visitor to a foreign country. For a school report, write about what you saw and did as a visitor. What things did you find the same or different? Write a short report below using six spelling words..

_____

_____

_____

_____

_____

_____

_____

Words with Double Consonants

Look at the words in each set. One word in each set is spelled correctly.
Use a pencil to color in the circle in front of that word. Before you begin,
look at the sample sets of words. Sample A has been done for you.
Do Sample B by yourself. When you are sure you know what to do,
you may go on with the rest of the page.

Sample A
- Ⓐ peble
- ⬤B pebble
- Ⓒ pebbal
- Ⓓ pebul

Sample B
- Ⓔ slipper
- Ⓕ sliper
- Ⓖ slippur
- Ⓗ slyper

1.
- Ⓐ unhappy
- Ⓑ unhappey
- Ⓒ unnhapy
- Ⓓ unhapey

2.
- Ⓔ ruber
- Ⓕ rubbur
- Ⓖ rubbor
- Ⓗ rubber

3.
- Ⓐ sily
- Ⓑ siley
- Ⓒ silley
- Ⓓ silly

4.
- Ⓔ midle
- Ⓕ middel
- Ⓖ middle
- Ⓗ mittle

5.
- Ⓐ gras
- Ⓑ grasss
- Ⓒ grasse
- Ⓓ grass

6.
- Ⓔ ribin
- Ⓕ ribbon
- Ⓖ ribben
- Ⓗ ribban

7.
- Ⓐ butter
- Ⓑ budder
- Ⓒ buttar
- Ⓓ buttor

8.
- Ⓔ hobey
- Ⓕ hobby
- Ⓖ hobbey
- Ⓗ hobbie

9.
- Ⓐ suppre
- Ⓑ suppor
- Ⓒ supar
- Ⓓ supper

10.
- Ⓔ smaul
- Ⓕ smawll
- Ⓖ smal
- Ⓗ small

11.
- Ⓐ lader
- Ⓑ ladder
- Ⓒ latter
- Ⓓ laddar

12.
- Ⓔ leson
- Ⓕ lesson
- Ⓖ lescon
- Ⓗ lesun

13.
- Ⓐ posible
- Ⓑ possibul
- Ⓒ possible
- Ⓓ possuble

14.
- Ⓔ happun
- Ⓕ hapin
- Ⓖ happn
- Ⓗ happen

15.
- Ⓐ litel
- Ⓑ littul
- Ⓒ little
- Ⓓ litle

Grade 3.1/Unit 3
The Little Painter of Sabana Grande
15

Words with /ou/ and /oi/

Pretest Directions

Fold back the paper along the dotted line. Use the blanks to write each word as it is read aloud. When you finish the test, unfold the paper. Use the list at the right to correct any spelling mistakes. Practice the words you missed for the Posttest.

To Parents

Here are the results of your child's weekly spelling Pretest. You can help your child study for the Posttest by following these simple steps for each word on the word list:

1. Read the word to your child.

2. Have your child write the word, saying each letter as it is written.

3. Say each letter of the word as your child checks the spelling.

4. If a mistake has been made, have your child read each letter of the correctly spelled word aloud, and then repeat steps 1-3.

1. _____ 1. found
2. _____ 2. spoil
3. _____ 3. power
4. _____ 4. enjoy
5. _____ 5. foil
6. _____ 6. clown
7. _____ 7. voyage
8. _____ 8. cloudy
9. _____ 9. noisy
10. _____ 10. count
11. _____ 11. poison
12. _____ 12. loyal
13. _____ 13. allow
14. _____ 14. choice
15. _____ 15. shout

Challenge Words

_____ anxious
_____ attic
_____ costume
_____ examined
_____ pattern

Words with /ou/ and /oi/

Using the Word Study Steps

1. LOOK at the word.

2. SAY the word aloud.

3. STUDY the letters in the wor

4. WRITE the word.

5. CHECK the word.
   Did you spell the word right?
   If not, go back to step 1.

Spelling Tip

- The sound /oi/ in the middle of the a word or syllable is usually spelled **oi**; at the end it is usually spelled **oy**.

- The sound /ou/ at the end of a word or syllable is spelled **ow**.

Circle the Rhyming Word

Circle the word that rhymes with the word in dark type.

power	poison	tower	pear
clown	allow	cloudy	town
spoil	foil	pail	spill
loyal	noisy	enjoy	royal
shout	out	shot	short
count	coat	mount	moth
choice	voice	voyage	enjoy
voyage	doe	do	drew

To Parents or Helpers:
      Using the Word Study Steps above as your child comes across any new words will help him or her spell well. Review the steps as you both go over this week's spelling words.
      Go over each Spelling Tip with your child. Point out the spelling words that follow the pattern. Help your child complete the spelling activity.

McGraw-Hill School Division

Words with /ou/ and /oi/

found	enjoy	voyage	count	allow
spoil	foil	cloudy	poison	choice
power	clown	noisy	loyal	shout

Pattern Power

Write the spelling words with the /ou/ sound spelled:

ou

1. _____
2. _____
3. _____
4. _____

ow

5. _____
6. _____
7. _____

Write the spelling words with the /oi/ sound spelled:

oi

8. _____
9. _____
10. _____
11. _____
12. _____

oy

13. _____
14. _____
15. _____

Syllable Stuff

Find spelling words that have one syllable:

16. _____   17. _____   18. _____

19. _____   20. _____   21. _____

22. _____

Find spelling words that have two syllables:

23. _____   24. _____   25. _____

26. _____   27. _____   28. _____

29. _____   30. _____

Words with /ou/ and /oi/

found	enjoy	voyage	count	allow
spoil	foil	cloudy	poison	choice
power	clown	noisy	loyal	shout

Analogies

An **analogy** is a statement that compares sets of words that are alike in some way.   Use spelling words to complete the analogies below.

1. *Dark* is to *light* as *silent* is to _____.

2. *Jolly* is to *merry* as *let* is to _____.

3. *Ship* is to *boat* as *trip* is to _____.

4. *Night* is to *day* as *lost* is to _____.

5. *Up* is to *down* as *whisper* is to _____.

6. *Dull* is to *shiny* as *sunny* is to _____.

A Fine Definition

Fill in the spelling word that matches the definition.

7. be happy with _____   **8.** thin metal sheet _____

9. say numbers in order _____   **10.** faithful _____

11. a silly performer _____   **12.** a chance to decide _____

13. strength or force _____   **14.** harmful or deadly _____

15. to ruin or damage _____

Challenge Extension: Have students write a fill in the blank sentence for each Challenge Word, then exchange papers with a partner and complete each other's sentences.

80

Book 3.1/Unit 3
The Patchwork Quilt
15

McGraw-Hill School Division

Words with /ou/ and /oi/

Proofreading Paragraph

There are six spelling mistakes in this letter. Circle the misspelled words.
Write the words correctly on the lines below.

Dear President:

    I am writing this letter to let you know about your toy cloun. I bought a
Happy Face toy yesterday. But when I took the toy out of the box, I saw
that it was broken. Boy, did it ever spoyle my day!

    I used to be a loyle customer of Happy Face toys. However, now my
Mom and Dad won't alow me to buy another one of your toys.

    Now all I want is my money back. I hope I can counte on you to do the
right thing. Since you are the president of the company, I know you have
the powre to do it. Thank you.

                    Sincerely,

                    Marcy Shore

1. _____ 2. _____ 3. _____

4. _____ 5. _____ 6. _____

Writing Activity

Did you ever have a toy spoil your day? What went wrong? Write several
sentences explaining what happened. Use six spelling words and circle
them.

_____

_____

_____

_____

_____

Words with /ou/ and /oi/

Look at the words in each set. One word in each set is spelled correctly.
Use a pencil to color in the circle in front of that word. Before you begin,
look at the sample sets of words. Sample A has been done for you.
Do Sample B by yourself. When you are sure you know what to do,
you may go on with the rest of the page.

Sample A
Ⓐ boyle
Ⓑ boile
Ⓒ boyalt
Ⓔ boil

Sample B
Ⓔ toun
Ⓕ toune
Ⓖ town
Ⓗ towne

1. Ⓐ spoyl
   Ⓑ spoil
   Ⓒ spole
   Ⓓ spoyal

2. Ⓔ noyzy
   Ⓕ nousy
   Ⓖ noisy
   Ⓗ noizee

3. Ⓐ loiyal
   Ⓑ loyle
   Ⓒ loyel
   Ⓓ loyal

4. Ⓔ choice
   Ⓕ choyce
   Ⓖ choice
   Ⓗ choise

5. Ⓐ fole
   Ⓑ foil
   Ⓒ foyal
   Ⓓ foile

6. Ⓔ foud
   Ⓕ found
   Ⓖ fown
   Ⓗ fownd

7. Ⓐ posin
   Ⓑ poizon
   Ⓒ poisun
   Ⓓ poison

8. Ⓔ voiage
   Ⓕ voyaj
   Ⓖ voyage
   Ⓗ voiag

9. Ⓐ shout
   Ⓑ shhout
   Ⓒ showt
   Ⓓ sout

10. Ⓔ alow
    Ⓕ allow
    Ⓖ alou
    Ⓗ allou

11. Ⓐ cout
    Ⓑ cownt
    Ⓒ count
    Ⓓ counte

12. Ⓔ powa
    Ⓕ pore
    Ⓖ power
    Ⓗ powor

13. Ⓐ kloudy
    Ⓑ cloudy
    Ⓒ clody
    Ⓓ cloude

14. Ⓔ clown
    Ⓕ klown
    Ⓖ clon
    Ⓗ kloun

15. Ⓐ enjoy
    Ⓑ injoy
    Ⓒ enjoe
    Ⓓ engoy

McGraw-Hill School Division

Adding *-ed* and *-ing*

Pretest Directions

Fold back the paper along the dotted line. Use the blanks to write each word as it is read aloud. When you finish the test, unfold the paper. Use the list at the right to correct any spelling mistakes. Practice the words you missed for the Posttest.

To Parents

Here are the results of your child's weekly spelling Pretest. You can help your child study for the Posttest by following these simple steps for each word on the word list:

1. Read the word to your child.

2. Have your child write the word, saying each letter as it is written.

3. Say each letter of the word as your child checks the spelling.

4. If a mistake has been made, have your child read each letter of the correctly spelled word aloud, and then repeat steps 1-3.

1. _____	1. spied
2. _____	2. moving
3. _____	3. robbed
4. _____	4. saving
5. _____	5. blamed
6. _____	6. beginning
7. _____	7. fried
8. _____	8. shaking
9. _____	9. supplied
10. _____	10. buried
11. _____	11. escaping
12. _____	12. hurried
13. _____	13. stirred
14. _____	14. splitting
15. _____	15. divided

Challenge Words

_____ combine

_____ invented

_____ located

_____ prairie

_____ wilderness

Name_____ Date_____

Adding *-ed* and *-ing*

Using the Word Study Steps

1. LOOK at the word.

2. SAY the word aloud.

3. STUDY the letters in the wor

4. WRITE the word.

5. CHECK the word.
   Did you spell the word right?
   If not, go back to step 1.

Spelling Tip

• When words end in silent **e**, drop the **e** when adding an ending that begins with a vowel.

 sav**e** - **e** + **ing** = **saving**

• When a word ends with a consonant followed by **y**, change the **y** to **i** when adding any ending except endings that begin with **i**.

 sp**y** + **es** = sp**ies**

• When a one-syllable word ends in one vowel followed by one consonant, double the consonant before adding an ending that begins with a vowel.

 begin + **ing** = begin**ning**

X the Word

Put an x on the word that does not belong in each row.

rubbed	stirred	matched	grabbed
moving	saving	shaking	playing
lined	supplied	buried	spied
beginning	splitting	running	counting
hurried	blamed	decided	divided

To Parents or Helpers:
   Using the Word Study Steps above as your child comes across any new words will help him or her spell well. Review the steps as you both go over this week's spelling words.
   Go over each Spelling Tip with your child. Help your child find other spelling words that follow each rule.
   Help your child complete the spelling activity.

Grade 3.1/Unit 3
Pecos Bill 5

McGraw-Hill School Division

Adding *-ed* and *-ing*

spied	saving	fried	buried	stirred
moving	blamed	shaking	escaping	splitting
robbed	beginning	supplied	hurried	divided

Pattern Power

Write the spelling words that show what you do before adding *–ed* and *–ing*.

double final consonant   **drop e**   **change y to i**

1. _____   5. _____   11. _____

2. _____   6. _____   12. _____

3. _____   7. _____   13. _____

4. _____   8. _____   14. _____

                                              9. _____   15. _____

                                             10. _____

Order, Please!

Write each group of spelling words in alphabetical order.

spied, saving, shaking, stirred

16. _____   17. _____

18. _____   19. _____

blamed, divided, escaping, beginning, buried

20. _____   21. _____

22. _____   23. _____

24. _____

Adding -ed and -ing

spied	saving	fried	buried	stirred
moving	blamed	shaking	escaping	splitting
robbed	beginning	supplied	hurried	divided

Finish the Sentence

Use spelling words to complete each sentence.

1. The thief _____ me of my wallet!

2. The title page is at the _____ of a book.

3. We had _____ chicken for dinner last night.

4. When Jay woke up late, he _____ to get to school on time.

5. My family and I are _____ to a new home in Florida.

6. Our teacher _____ us with paints for the art project.

7. The prisoner was caught _____ from jail.

8. Alicia _____ the ribbons into blue ones and red ones.

Find the Base Words

Write the base word of these *–ed* words:

9. spied _____   10. robbed _____

11. blamed _____   12. fried _____

Write the base word of these *–ing* words:

13. splitting _____   14. shaking _____

15. beginning _____   16. escaping _____

Challenge Extension: Ask students to write a short
paragraph that includes each Challenge Word.

McGraw-Hill School Division

Adding *-ed* and *-ing*

Proofreading Paragraph

There are six spelling mistakes in this paragraph. Circle the misspelled words. Write the words correctly on the lines below.

Two men robed a bank. They berryed all but one of the sacks of money. They devided the rest of the money equally between the two of them.

When the two men reached the next town, they stopped. "I smell fryed chicken," said Luke. "Let's eat!" So the hungry men hurried into a small coffee shop and ordered everything on the menu. But when the time came to pay the bill, neither of the robbers wanted to pay.

"Come on, Luke, pay up!" said Bart. What are you sayving it for?"

"Why should I pay?" asked Luke.

While the two men were busy arguing, the sheriff and his deputies walked in. Each blammed the other for their bad luck.

1. _____ 2. _____ 3. _____

4. _____ 5. _____ 6. _____

Writing Activity

Write a short story that takes place in the old west. How does the story begin? What do the characters do? How does the story end? Use six spelling words.

_____

_____

_____

_____

_____

McGraw-Hill School Division

Adding *-ed* and *-ing*

Look at the words in each set. One word in each set is spelled correctly.
Use a pencil to color in the circle in front of that word. Before you begin,
look at the sample sets of words. Sample A has been done for you.
Do Sample B by yourself. When you are sure you know what to do,
you may go on with the rest of the page.

Sample A
- (A) tried
- (B) tryed
- (C) treid
- (D) tride

Sample B
- (E) caried
- (F) carryed
- (G) caryed
- (H) carried

1.
- (A) devided
- (B) divided
- (C) divyded
- (D) deivided

2.
- (E) fried
- (F) fryed
- (G) freid
- (H) fride

3.
- (A) ciplied
- (B) suplied
- (C) supplied
- (D) sepplied

4.
- (E) movin
- (F) mooving
- (G) movving
- (H) moving

5.
- (A) begining
- (B) beginning
- (C) beggining
- (D) begineng

6.
- (E) robed
- (F) robbed
- (G) rawbed
- (H) raubed

7.
- (A) stird
- (B) stirred
- (C) stired
- (D) sturred

8.
- (E) eskaping
- (F) escayping
- (G) eschaping
- (H) escaping

9.
- (A) hurryed
- (B) hurried
- (C) herried
- (D) huried

10.
- (E) blaymed
- (F) blaimed
- (G) blamed
- (H) blamde

11.
- (A) spyed
- (B) spied
- (C) spide
- (D) spyde

12.
- (E) shaking
- (F) shacking
- (G) shakin
- (H) schaking

13.
- (A) buryed
- (B) berried
- (C) barried
- (D) buried

14.
- (E) splittin
- (F) sppliting
- (G) splitting
- (H) splytting

15.
- (A) saiving
- (B) savving
- (C) saving
- (D) sayving

McGraw-Hill School Division

Words from Science

Pretest Directions

Fold back the paper along the dotted line. Use the blanks to write each word as it is read aloud. When you finish the test, unfold the paper. Use the list at the right to correct any spelling mistakes. Practice the words you missed for the Posttest.

To Parents

Here are the results of your child's weekly spelling Pretest. You can help your child study for the Posttest by following these simple steps for each word on the word list:

1. Read the word to your child.

2. Have your child write the word, saying each letter as it is written.

3. Say each letter of the word as your child checks the spelling.

4. If a mistake has been made, have your child read each letter of the correctly spelled word aloud, and then repeat steps 1-3.

1. _____	1. ice
2. _____	2. solid
3. _____	3. melt
4. _____	4. northern
5. _____	5. heat
6. _____	6. freezes
7. _____	7. matter
8. _____	8. frost
9. _____	9. snowflake
10. _____	10. thaw
11. _____	11. arctic
12. _____	12. dense
13. _____	13. degree
14. _____	14. chill
15. _____	15. igloo

Challenge Words

_____ beauty

_____ furniture

_____ palace

_____ pure

_____ visitors

Words from Science

Using the Word Study Steps

1. LOOK at the word.

2. SAY the word aloud.

3. STUDY the letters in the wor

4. WRITE the word.

5. CHECK the word.
   Did you spell the word right?
   If not, go back to step 1.

Spelling Tip

Make up clues to help you remember the spelling.

It's c--**c**--cold in the arctic! (Don't forget the **c** in the middle of ar**c**tic.

Find and Circle

Where are the spelling words?

```
s  n  o  w  f  l  a  k  e  e  n  o  r  t  h  e  r  n
o  m  e  l  t  c  f  r  e  e  z  e  s  l  t  h  a  w
l  f  r  o  s  t  r  i  c  e  x  d  e  g  r  e  e  y
i  g  l  o  o  q  a  r  c  t  i  c  b  d  e  n  s  e
d  m  a  t  t  e  r  u  c  h  i  l  l  r  h  e  a  t
```

To Parents or Helpers:

Using the Word Study Steps above as your child comes across any new words will help him or her spell well. Review the steps as you both go over this week's spelling words.

Go over the Spelling Tip with your child. Help him or her think of other clues that will help to remember the spelling of new words.

Help your child find and circle the spelling words in the puzzle.

Words from Science

ice	northern	matter	thaw	degree
solid	heat	frost	arctic	chill
melt	freezes	snowflake	dense	igloo

Pattern Power

Write the spelling words that have one syllable.

1. _____ 2. _____ 3. _____

4. _____ 5. _____ 6. _____

7. _____

Write the spelling words that have two syllables.

8. _____ 9. _____ 10. _____

11. _____ 12. _____ 13. _____

14. _____ 15. _____

Rhyme Time

Write a spelling word that rhymes with each of these words

16. fatter _____   17. claw _____

18. sense _____   19. lost _____

20. seat _____   21. sneezes _____

Word Scramble

Unscramble each spelling word

22. nowesfakl __ __ __ __ __ __ __ __ __

23. ologi __ __ __ __ __

24. edgere __ __ __ __ __ __

25. iec __ __ __

Words from Science

ice	northern	matter	thaw	degree
solid	heat	frost	arctic	chill
melt	freezes	snowflake	dense	igloo

A Clue for You
Write the spelling word that fits the clue.

1. opposite of southern _____

2. a house made of ice _____

3. if butter gets too warm it will do this _____

4. when cold water changes to a solid _____

5. ice crystal in air _____

6. area at the top of the world _____

7. before you cook frozen meat it must do this _____

8. ice crystals that you can see on windows _____

Fill in the Blanks
Write the list word that completes each sentence.

9. Janice wore her sweater when she felt a _____ in the air.

10. The car skidded on a patch of _____ on the road.

11. It doesn't _____ to me whether it rains or snows tomorrow.

12. The fog was so _____ it was hard to see the road.

13. When water freezes it changes from a liquid to a _____.

14. A wood-burning fireplace provides _____.

15. The temperature today is only one _____ warmer than yesterday.

Word Journal
One of your spelling words is *arctic*. Write about some things that happen in arctic weather.

_____

_____

_____

Challenge Extension: Have students write each Challenge Word and then circle each syllable. Have them check their work in a dictionary.

Grade 3.1/Unit 3
A Very Cool Place to Visit 15

McGraw-Hill School Division

Words from Science

Proofreading Paragraph

There are six spelling mistakes in this weather report. Circle the misspelled words. Write the words correctly on the lines below.

In the northarn states, the weather will be quite cold tomorrow. The temperature may even reach one digre below zero. Now that's artic weather! This chill will last for several days. Anyone care to build an iglo?

Now, there's another mattir to report. Our friends down south, of course, have a different weather problem. They are complaining about the hete!

1. _____ 2. _____ 3. _____

4. _____ 5. _____ 6. _____

Writing Activity

What questions would you like to ask someone who lives in a very cold climate? Write your interview questions, using at least six spelling words.

_____

_____

_____

_____

_____

McGraw-Hill School Division

Words from Science

Look at the words in each set. One word in each set is spelled correctly.
Use a pencil to color in the circle in front of that word. Before you begin,
look at the sample sets of words. Sample A has been done for you.
Do Sample B by yourself. When you are sure you know what to do,
you may go on with the rest of the page.

Sample A
Ⓐ spil
🅑 spill
Ⓒ spile
Ⓓ spille

Sample B
Ⓔ sothern
Ⓕ suthern
Ⓖ southern
Ⓗ southurn

1. Ⓐ taw
   Ⓑ thawe
   Ⓒ thaw
   Ⓓ thow

2. Ⓔ chil
   Ⓕ chill
   Ⓖ chille
   Ⓗ chell

3. Ⓐ heat
   Ⓑ heet
   Ⓒ hete
   Ⓓ heyt

4. Ⓔ eyce
   Ⓕ ise
   Ⓖ ice
   Ⓗ iece

5. Ⓐ snowflake
   Ⓑ snoflake
   Ⓒ snowflace
   Ⓓ snowfake

6. Ⓔ solid
   Ⓕ solled
   Ⓖ sullid
   Ⓗ solide

7. Ⓐ mellt
   Ⓑ melet
   Ⓒ mellet
   Ⓓ melt

8. Ⓔ frawst
   Ⓕ frast
   Ⓖ forst
   Ⓗ frost

9. Ⓐ dence
   Ⓑ dens
   Ⓒ dense
   Ⓓ deanse

10. Ⓔ iglu
    Ⓕ igloo
    Ⓖ iglue
    Ⓗ ickloo

11. Ⓐ northern
    Ⓑ nothern
    Ⓒ northurn
    Ⓓ norturn

12. Ⓔ arctic
    Ⓕ artic
    Ⓖ arktic
    Ⓗ artick

13. Ⓐ freeses
    Ⓑ freecez
    Ⓒ freazes
    Ⓓ freezes

14. Ⓔ dagree
    Ⓕ degree
    Ⓖ digree
    Ⓗ diggrea

15. Ⓐ maturr
    Ⓑ matter
    Ⓒ mattar
    Ⓓ matture

Book 3.1/Unit 3 Review Test

Read each sentence. If an underlined word is spelled wrong, fill in the circle that
goes with that word. If no word is spelled wrong, fill in the circle below NONE.
Read Sample A, and do Sample B.

A. He <u>hoped</u> that his <u>singing</u> was <u>bettur</u>.
     A   B   C

NONE
A. Ⓐ Ⓑ ● Ⓓ

B. Tom <u>worried</u> about <u>making</u> the <u>dinner</u>.
          E   F   G

NONE
B. Ⓔ Ⓕ Ⓖ Ⓗ

1. I want to <u>thank</u> my <u>friend</u> for the <u>silly</u> song.
            A   B   C

NONE
1. Ⓐ Ⓑ Ⓒ Ⓓ

2. Maria <u>spied</u> a <u>noisy</u> squirrel on the <u>ladder</u>.
          E   F   G

NONE
2. Ⓔ Ⓕ Ⓖ Ⓗ

3. Joey <u>hurryed</u> to <u>thank</u> the man for the <u>butter</u>.
        A   B   C

NONE
3. Ⓐ Ⓑ Ⓒ Ⓓ

4. I heard a <u>noisy</u> <u>shout</u> when the thief <u>robed</u> the store.
           E   F   G

NONE
4. Ⓔ Ⓕ Ⓖ Ⓗ

5. Did you <u>enjoy</u> <u>supper</u> with your <u>freind</u>?
          A   B   C

NONE
5. Ⓐ Ⓑ Ⓒ Ⓓ

6. The <u>heet</u> and <u>power</u> went out in the <u>northern</u> area.
         E   F   G

NONE
6. Ⓔ Ⓕ Ⓖ Ⓗ

7. He will climb the <u>ladder</u> and <u>paint</u> on a <u>cloudey</u> day.
             A   B   C

NONE
7. Ⓐ Ⓑ Ⓒ Ⓓ

8. I <u>belong</u> in a <u>northern</u> state where water <u>freazes</u>.
     E   F   G

NONE
8. Ⓔ Ⓕ Ⓖ Ⓗ

9. Mark made a <u>noizy</u> <u>thump</u> when he was <u>moving</u>.
            A   B   C

NONE
9. Ⓐ Ⓑ Ⓒ Ⓓ

10. I will not <u>enjoy</u> the ice cream if you <u>melt</u> it on the <u>heat</u>.
           E   F   G

NONE
10. Ⓔ Ⓕ Ⓖ Ⓗ

Go on

McGraw-Hill School Division

11. Susan is <u>moveing</u> the <u>paint</u> and the <u>ladder</u>.
          A   B   C

NONE
11. Ⓐ Ⓑ Ⓒ Ⓓ

12. Will a <u>snowflak</u> <u>melt</u> if it's near <u>heat</u>?
          E   F   G

NONE
12. Ⓔ Ⓕ Ⓖ Ⓗ

13. Let's <u>shout</u> the <u>silly</u>, <u>noisey</u> song!
         A   B   C

NONE
13. Ⓐ Ⓑ Ⓒ Ⓓ

14. Frank and Jim <u>enjoy</u> <u>butter</u> with their <u>soupper</u>.
             E   F   G

NONE
14. Ⓔ Ⓕ Ⓖ Ⓗ

15. I <u>engoy</u> <u>shaking</u> the gift tied with a <u>ribbon</u>.
     A   B   C

NONE
15. Ⓐ Ⓑ Ⓒ Ⓓ

16. It was <u>cloudy</u> the day he <u>spyed</u> the silly <u>goose</u>.
        E   F   G

NONE
16. Ⓔ Ⓕ Ⓖ Ⓗ

17. The electric <u>power</u> freezer <u>freezes</u> his <u>butter</u>.
           A   B   C

NONE
17. Ⓐ Ⓑ Ⓒ Ⓓ

18. Did you <u>paint</u> a <u>silly</u> <u>ribban</u> in her hair?
         E   F   G

NONE
18. Ⓔ Ⓕ Ⓖ Ⓗ

19. We <u>enjoy</u> <u>shakeing</u> the apples because they <u>thump</u>.
     A   B   C

NONE
19. Ⓐ Ⓑ Ⓒ Ⓓ

20. <u>Shout</u> a <u>noisy</u> word when it's time for <u>suppir</u>.
   E   F   G

NONE
20. Ⓔ Ⓕ Ⓖ Ⓗ

21. Steven <u>spied</u> a <u>ribbun</u> tied to the <u>ladder</u>.
        A   B   C

NONE
21. Ⓐ Ⓑ Ⓒ Ⓓ

22. Who <u>robbed</u> my <u>friend</u> and took her <u>paynt</u>?
      E   F   G

NONE
22. Ⓔ Ⓕ Ⓖ Ⓗ

23. If the <u>powur</u> goes out the <u>butter</u> will <u>melt</u>.
      A   B   C

NONE
23. Ⓐ Ⓑ Ⓒ Ⓓ

24. If you <u>belong</u> to the <u>Noisy</u> Club you can <u>shout</u>!
     E   F   G

NONE
24. Ⓔ Ⓕ Ⓖ Ⓗ

25. Bob <u>hurried</u> up the <u>latter</u> and began to <u>paint</u>.
      A   B   C

NONE
25. Ⓐ Ⓑ Ⓒ Ⓓ

McGraw-Hill School Division

Words with *th, wh, ch, sh*

Pretest Directions

Fold back the paper along the dotted line. Use the blanks to write each word as it is read aloud. When you finish the test, unfold the paper. Use the list at the right to correct any spelling mistakes. Practice the words you missed for the Posttest.

To Parents

Here are the results of your child's weekly spelling Pretest. You can help your child study for the Posttest by following these simple steps for each word on the word list:

1. Read the word to your child.

2. Have your child write the word, saying each letter as it is written.

3. Say each letter of the word as your child checks the spelling.

4. If a mistake has been made, have your child read each letter of the correctly spelled word aloud, and then repeat steps 1-3.

1. _____ 1. shadow
2. _____ 2. thirsty
3. _____ 3. whip
4. _____ 4. cherry
5. _____ 5. thick
6. _____ 6. shock
7. _____ 7. cheese
8. _____ 8. whisker
9. _____ 9. thousand
10. _____ 10. shone
11. _____ 11. chain
12. _____ 12. whether
13. _____ 13. thirty
14. _____ 14. chicken
15. _____ 15. shelf

Challenge Words

_____ completely
_____ humans
_____ motion
_____ reply
_____ weight

Words with *th*, *wh*, *ch*, *sh*

Using the Word Study Steps

1. LOOK at the word.

2. SAY the word aloud.

3. STUDY the letters in the word.

4. WRITE the word.

5. CHECK the word.
   Did you spell the word right?
   If not, go back to step 1.

Spelling Tip

Think of times you may have seen the word in reading, on signs, or in a textbook. Try to remember how it looked. Write the word in different ways. Which one looks correct?

~~chiken~~ ~~chickin~~ chicken

Word Scramble

Unscramble each set of letters to make a spelling word.

1. hawdos _____

2. rtysiht _____

3. piwh _____

4. ryerch _____

5. cikht _____

6. khosc _____

7. eshece _____

8. skirihw _____

9. uadhotsn _____

10. neosh _____

11. incha _____

12. eterwhh _____

13. yhttri _____

14. enccikh _____

15. flehs _____

To Parents or Helpers:
Using the Word Study Steps above as your child comes across any new words will help him or her spell well. Review the steps as you both go over this week's spelling words.
Go over the Spelling Tip with your child. Help your child write some of the spelling words in different ways to figure out which one looks correct.
Help your child complete the spelling activity.

Book 3,2/Unit 1
The Terrible EEK 15

Words with *th, wh, ch, sh*

shadow	cherry	cheese	shone	thirty
thirsty	thick	whisker	chain	chicken
whip	shock	thousand	whether	shelf

Write the spelling words with these spelling patterns.

th

1. _____

2. _____

3. _____

4. _____

wh

5. _____

6. _____

7. _____

ch

8. _____

9. _____

10. _____

11. _____

sh

12. _____

13. _____

14. _____

15. _____

Sounds Alike

Write the spelling word that rhymes with each word below.

16. chip _____

17. sick _____

18. clock _____

19. berry _____

20. self _____

Words with *th*, *wh*, *ch*, *sh*

shadow	cherry	cheese	shone	thirty
thirsty	thick	whisker	chain	chicken
whip	shock	thousand	whether	shelf

Complete each sentence below with a spelling word or words.

1. The bike had a lock and a _____.

2. Ten times one hundred is one _____.

3. The light _____ through the window.

4. I don't know _____ I'll be able to come to your party.

5. I looked for the book on the _____.

6. Sally asked for a _____ on top of her ice cream.

7. Mom will _____ the cream for the top of the pie.

8. In cold weather, you can get a _____ when you touch metal.

9. We saw a _____ at the farm.

10. I cannot see my _____ on a cloudy day.

Invention Connection

Create a mousetrap. Use the spelling words: *cherry*, *cheese*, *thick*, *thirty*, and *whisper* to describe how the trap will catch the mouse.

_____

_____

_____

_____

Challenge Extension: Have students write fill-in sentences for each challenge word. Then have each student exchange his sentences with a partner and see how many the other student can correctly fill in.

100

Book 3,2/Unit 1
The Terrible EEK 15

McGraw-Hill School Division

Words with *th*, *wh*, *ch*, *sh*

Proofreading

There are six spelling mistakes in the letter below. Circle the misspelled words. Write the words correctly on the lines below.

Dear Tom,

    I was so happy to get your letter! I didn't know wether or not you would write to me. I bet you were really thursty after picking strawberries, especially if the hot sun showen all day. Will you wip some cream to put on them? Thanks for the cheeze from your parents' farm. It was delicious. I had a thik slice on a sandwich for lunch.

Your friend,

Elizabeth

1. _____ 2. _____ 3. _____

4. _____ 5. _____ 6. _____

Writing Activity

Imagine you are a scientist who has just discovered life on another planet. Send a fax to your assistant about your exciting news. Use four spelling words.

_____

_____

_____

_____

_____

Words with *th*, *wh*, *ch*, *sh*

Look at the words in each set. One word in each set is spelled correctly.
Use a pencil to color in the circle in front of that word. Before you begin,
look at the sample sets of words. Sample A has been done for you.
Do Sample B by yourself. When you are sure you know what to do,
you may go on with the rest of the page.

Sample A
- (A) babees
- (B) babys
- (C) babies ●
- (D) babeez

Sample B
- (E) chaking
- (F) shaking
- (G) schaking
- (H) saking

1.
- (A) thursty
- (B) thersty
- (C) thirsty
- (D) thirstee

2.
- (E) chery
- (F) cherrie
- (G) cherie
- (H) cherry

3.
- (A) shok
- (B) shock
- (C) schock
- (D) shoke

4.
- (A) whisker
- (F) wisker
- (G) whiskir
- (H) whiska

5.
- (A) shoon
- (B) shone
- (C) schone
- (D) showen

6.
- (E) wheather
- (F) whetha
- (G) weatha
- (H) whether

7.
- (A) chicken
- (B) chiken
- (C) chikin
- (D) chickin

8.
- (E) chelf
- (F) shelfe
- (G) shelf
- (H) shelff

9.
- (A) therty
- (B) thurty
- (C) thirtee
- (D) thirty

10.
- (E) chayne
- (F) chain
- (G) chane
- (H) chaine

11.
- (A) thousand
- (B) thousend
- (C) tousand
- (D) thosand

12.
- (E) cheez
- (F) chease
- (G) cheese
- (H) chese

13.
- (A) thicke
- (B) thick
- (C) thik
- (D) thike

14.
- (E) wip
- (F) whipe
- (G) wipp
- (H) whip

15.
- (A) shadow
- (B) shadoe
- (C) shado
- (D) shatow

Book 3,2/Unit 1
The Terrible EEK
15

McGraw-Hill School Division

Words with *ch*, *tch*, *sh*, *th*

Pretest Directions

Fold back the paper along the dotted line. Use the blanks to write each word as it is read aloud. When you finish the test, unfold the paper. Use the list at the right to correct any spelling mistakes. Practice the words you missed for the Posttest.

To Parents

Here are the results of your child's weekly spelling Pretest. You can help your child study for the Posttest by following these simple steps for each word on the word list:

1. Read the word to your child.

2. Have your child write the word, saying each letter as it is written.

3. Say each letter of the word as your child checks the spelling.

4. If a mistake has been made, have your child read each letter of the correctly spelled word aloud, and then repeat steps 1-3.

1. _____	1. splash
2. _____	2. fetch
3. _____	3. tooth
4. _____	4. teach
5. _____	5. itch
6. _____	6. peach
7. _____	7. fourth
8. _____	8. crash
9. _____	9. coach
10. _____	10. sketch
11. _____	11. finish
12. _____	12. underneath
13. _____	13. stitch
14. _____	14. squash
15. _____	15. approach

Challenge Words

_____	comforting
_____	designed
_____	dozens
_____	encouraging
_____	relatives

Words with *ch*, *tch*, *sh*, *th*

Using the Word Study Steps

1. LOOK at the word.

2. SAY the word aloud.

3. STUDY the letters in the word.

4. WRITE the word.

5. CHECK the word.
   Did you spell the word right?
   If not, go back to step 1.

Spelling Tip

• If the **ch** sound immediately follows a short vowel in a one-syllable word, it is spelled **tch**. as in fe**tch**. There are a few exceptions in English: **much**, **such**, **which**, and **rich**.

• Divide the word into syllables.

    un   der   neath

Find and Circle

Where are the spelling words?

```
s p l a s h u t e a c h n f i n i s h c f
f o u r t h c s k e t c h l t o o t h r e
d p e a c h q u c o a c h u i t c h r a t
w a a p p r o a c h t h s q u a s h j s c
l s t i t c h z e d u n d e r n e a t h h
```

To Parents or Helpers:

Using the Word Study Steps above as your child comes across any new words will help him or her spell well. Review the steps as you both go over this week's spelling words.

Go over each Spelling Tip with your child. Ask him or her to find other new words that follow the rule concerning the **ch** sound. Help him or her divide other new words into syllables.

Help your child find and circle the spelling words in the puzzle.

McGraw-Hill School Division

Words with *ch, tch, sh, th*

splash	teach	fourth	sketch	stitch
fetch	itch	crash	finish	squash
tooth	peach	coach	underneath	approach

Pattern Power!

Write the spelling words for each spelling pattern.

ch

1. _____

2. _____

3. _____

4. _____

sh

9. _____

10. _____

11. _____

tch

5. _____

6. _____

7. _____

8. _____

th

12. _____

13. _____

14. _____

15. _____

Fill in the Blanks

Write the spelling words that completes each sentence.

16. A pair of words that both rhyme and end with *ash* are

_____ and _____.

17. The three words that contain long vowel sounds and end with *ch* are

_____, _____, and _____.

18. The three words that contain long vowel sounds and end in *tch* are

_____, _____, and _____.

19. The only two-syllable spelling words are _____ and

_____.

20. The only three-syllable spelling word is _____.

Words with *ch*, *tch*, *sh*, *th*

splash	teach	fourth	sketch	stitch
fetch	itch	crash	finish	squash
tooth	peach	coach	underneath	approach

Part of the Group

Read the heading for each group of words. Then add the spelling word that belongs in each group.

Fruits

1. apple, pear, _____

Order

2. second, third, _____

Parts of the Mouth

3. tongue, gums, _____

Pool Activities

4. swim, dive, _____

Dog Tricks

5. bark, heel, _____

Positions

6. above, on, _____

Vegetables

7. carrots, peas, _____

What Does it Mean?

Write the spelling word that has the same meaning as the word or phrase below.

8. loud sudden noise _____

9. complete _____

10. quick drawing _____

11. sew together _____

12. help _____

13. come closer _____

14. tickle, sting _____

15. help to learn _____

Challenge Extension: Have students make word search puzzles containing the challenge words. Then have students swap puzzles with a partner and solve the puzzle.

106

Book 3.2/Unit 1
In My Family 15

McGraw-Hill School Division

Words with *ch, tch, sh, th*

Proofreading

There are six spelling mistakes in the paragraph below. Circle the misspelled words. Write the words correctly on the lines below.

    Sometimes the swimming coch lets us splach around in the pool. My friend Maria likes to swim underneth the water. When we finnish swimming, we may go out for ice cream. My favorite flavor is peech. Often I go to a sewing club with some friends. We shop together for fabric and stich our own clothing.

1. _____ 2. _____ 3. _____

4. _____ 5. _____ 6. _____

Writing Activity

Write about something you like to do after school. Use four spelling words.

_____

_____

_____

_____

_____

Words with *ch*, *tch*, *sh*, *th*

Look at the words in each set. One word in each set is spelled correctly.
Use a pencil to color in the circle in front of that word. Before you begin,
look at the sample sets of words. Sample A has been done for you.
Do Sample B by yourself. When you are sure you know what to do,
you may go on with the rest of the page.

Sample A
- Ⓐ feesh
- Ⓑ fich
- ⬤ fish
- Ⓓ shish

Sample B
- Ⓔ wish
- Ⓕ wiss
- Ⓖ wich
- Ⓗ whith

1. Ⓐ approache
    Ⓑ approche
    Ⓒ approach
    Ⓓ aproach

2. Ⓕ stitch
    Ⓕ steetch
    Ⓖ steech
    Ⓗ stich

3. Ⓐ finitch
    Ⓑ finich
    Ⓒ finish
    Ⓓ finnisch

4. Ⓔ coche
    Ⓕ coach
    Ⓖ coache
    Ⓗ coatch

5. Ⓐ fourthe
    Ⓑ forthe
    Ⓒ firthe
    Ⓓ fourth

6. Ⓐ peach
    Ⓕ peech
    Ⓖ peetch
    Ⓗ peatch

7. Ⓐ ich
    Ⓑ itch
    Ⓒ itche
    Ⓓ eech

8. Ⓔ tuthe
    Ⓕ tooth
    Ⓖ toothe
    Ⓗ touth

9. Ⓐ splesh
    Ⓑ splash
    Ⓒ splish
    Ⓓ splashe

10. Ⓔ skwash
    Ⓕ skwash
    Ⓖ squash
    Ⓗ skwash

11. Ⓐ underneeth
    Ⓑ unduhneath
    Ⓒ underneath
    Ⓓ undeneat

12. Ⓐ teach
    Ⓕ teche
    Ⓖ teech
    Ⓗ teache

13. Ⓐ fehtch
    Ⓑ fech
    Ⓒ fetch
    Ⓓ fesh

14. Ⓔ skech
    Ⓕ sketch
    Ⓖ scetch
    Ⓗ scech

15. Ⓐ cratch
    Ⓑ krasch
    Ⓒ krash
    Ⓓ crash

McGraw-Hill School Division

Words with /ô/ and /ù/

Pretest Directions

Fold back the paper along the dotted line. Use the blanks to write each word as it is read aloud. When you finish the test, unfold the paper. Use the list at the right to correct any spelling mistakes. Practice the words you missed for the Posttest.

To Parents

Here are the results of your child's weekly spelling Pretest. You can help your child study for the Posttest by following these simple steps for each word on the word list:

1. Read the word to your child.

2. Have your child write the word, saying each letter as it is written.

3. Say each letter of the word as your child checks the spelling.

4. If a mistake has been made, have your child read each letter of the correctly spelled word aloud, and then repeat steps 1-3.

1. _____	1. woman
2. _____	2. tall
3. _____	3. cookie
4. _____	4. bought
5. _____	5. song
6. _____	6. pulls
7. _____	7. cause
8. _____	8. always
9. _____	9. wolf
10. _____	10. fought
11. _____	11. across
12. _____	12. sugar
13. _____	13. saucer
14. _____	14. often
15. _____	15. footprint

Challenge Words

_____	discovered
_____	insects
_____	remains
_____	tough
_____	treat

McGraw-Hill School Division

Words with /ô/ and /u̇/

Using the Word Study Steps

1. LOOK at the word.

2. SAY the word aloud.

3. STUDY the letters in the word.

4. WRITE the word.

5. CHECK the word.
   Did you spell the word right?
   If not, go back to step 1.

Spelling Tip

• Think of a word you know, such as a rhyming word, that has the same spelling pattern as the word you want to spell.

  b + ought = bought
  f + ought = fought

• Keep a Personal Word List in a notebook. Write words you have trouble spelling.

X the Word

Put an X on the word that does not rhyme with the word in dark type.

song	long	gong	wolf
bought	footprint	brought	fought
tall	halls	pulls	ball
often	soften	open	woman
across	cross	saucer	gross
sugar	always	cougar	burglar

To Parents or Helpers:

Using the Word Study Steps above as your child comes across any new words will help him or her spell well. Review the steps as you both go over this week's spelling words.

Go over each Spelling Tip with your child. Ask if he or she knows other words that rhyme with new words. Help your child write words that they have trouble spelling in a notebook that they can keep.

Help your child complete the spelling activity.

McGraw-Hill School Division

Words with /ô/ and /ů/

woman	bought	cause	fought	saucer
tall	song	always	across	often
cookie	pulls	wolf	sugar	footprint

This week's spelling words contain the vowel sounds /ô/ and /ů/. Write each spelling word under the word that has the same vowel sound spelled as shown. Then circle the letter or letters that spell the vowel sound in each word.

Word Sort

/ô/ spelled *a*

1. _____

2. _____

/ô/ spelled *0*

3. _____

4. _____

5. _____

/ô/ spelled *au*

6. _____

7. _____

/ô/ spelled *ough*

8. _____

9. _____

/ů/ spelled *oo*

10. _____

11. _____

/ů/ spelled *u*

12. _____

13. _____

/ů/ spelled *o*

14. _____

15. _____

Rhyme Time

Under each word, write a spelling word that rhymes with it.

long

16. _____

small

17. _____

pause

18. _____

Words with /ô/ and /u̇/

woman	bought	cause	fought	saucer
tall	song	always	across	often
cookie	pulls	wolf	sugar	footprint

What's the Word?

Complete each sentence with a spelling word.

1. Would you like a _____ to eat with your milk?

2. The hunter's boot left a very clear _____.

3. We _____ many gifts for our friends.

4. A _____ could be President of the United States.

5. How _____ do you go to the movies?

6. Alice thinks she isn't _____ enough to play on the basketball team.

7. They _____ send us a postcard when they go away on vacation.

8. Please put some water in the _____ for the cat.

9. I heard a great new _____ on the radio this morning.

10. The locomotive _____ the entire train.

11. A tame _____ was probably the ancestor of the dog.

12. If you _____ any more trouble, you'll be sent to the principal's office.

13. Would you like another lump of _____ in your tea?

14. We live _____ the road from a small grocery store.

15. The Battle of Gettysburg was _____ in the Civil War.

Synonym Alert!

Write the spelling words that have the same meanings as the words below.

16. purchased   _____

17. frequently   _____

18. struggled against   _____

Challenge Extension: Have students write one
sentence for each Challenge Word.

112

Book 3.2/Unit 1
Cactus Hotel 18

McGraw-Hill School Division

Words with /ô/ and /u̇/

Proofreading

There are six spelling mistakes in the paragraph below. Circle the misspelled words. Write the words correctly on the lines below.

Once upon a time, there was a tawl womun who lived in the forest. One day, she met a large gray wulf on the road. "Are you hungry," she asked. When the animal followed her home, she placed a cooky on an old sauser and left it in her backyard. After that day, she often saw the creature's futprint in the yard.

1. _____ 2. _____ 3. _____

4. _____ 5. _____ 6. _____

Writing Activity

Imagine that you have been asked to keep a group of first-graders entertained for a little while. Make up a funny story that might amuse them. Use four spelling words.

_____

_____

_____

_____

_____

Words with /ô/ and /ù/

Look at the words in each set. One word in each set is spelled correctly.
Use a pencil to color in the circle in front of that word. Before you begin,
look at the sample sets of words. Sample A has been done for you.
Do Sample B by yourself. When you are sure you know what to do,
you may go on with the rest of the page.

Sample A
- Ⓐ rong
- Ⓑ rongh
- Ⓒ wrong
- Ⓓ wron

Sample B
- Ⓔ tou
- Ⓕ tu
- Ⓖ tue
- Ⓗ too

1. Ⓐ talle
   Ⓑ taal
   Ⓒ thal
   Ⓓ tall

2. Ⓔ bawt
   Ⓕ bought
   Ⓖ boght
   Ⓗ baught

3. Ⓐ cuky
   Ⓑ kukky
   Ⓒ cookie
   Ⓓ cookee

4. Ⓐ woman
   Ⓕ womin
   Ⓖ wooman
   Ⓗ woomin

5. Ⓐ pulz
   Ⓑ pullse
   Ⓒ pulze
   Ⓓ pulls

6. Ⓐ song
   Ⓕ songe
   Ⓖ sawng
   Ⓗ songg

7. Ⓐ wulf
   Ⓑ wolf
   Ⓒ wolfe
   Ⓓ wulfe

8. Ⓔ shugar
   Ⓕ shuger
   Ⓖ sugar
   Ⓗ shuga

9. Ⓐ futprint
   Ⓑ footeprint
   Ⓒ foutprint
   Ⓓ footprint

10. Ⓐ often
    Ⓕ orfen
    Ⓖ offen
    Ⓗ oftin

11. Ⓐ sorcer
    Ⓑ saucer
    Ⓒ sawcer
    Ⓓ sauser

12. Ⓔ akross
    Ⓕ acros
    Ⓖ across
    Ⓗ acrost

13. Ⓐ fought
    Ⓑ faught
    Ⓒ forght
    Ⓓ fougt

14. Ⓔ alwayz
    Ⓕ alwase
    Ⓖ alwaze
    Ⓗ always

15. Ⓐ corse
    Ⓑ cause
    Ⓒ cours
    Ⓓ cauze

Compound Words

Pretest Directions

Fold back the paper along the dotted line. Use the blanks to write each word as it is read aloud. When you finish the test, unfold the paper. Use the list at the right to correct any spelling mistakes. Practice the words you missed for the Posttest.

To Parents

Here are the results of your child's weekly spelling Pretest. You can help your child study for the Posttest by following these simple steps for each word on the word list:

1. Read the word to your child.

2. Have your child write the word, saying each letter as it is written.

3. Say each letter of the word as your child checks the spelling.

4. If a mistake has been made, have your child read each letter of the correctly spelled word aloud, and then repeat steps 1-3.

1. _____ 1. everything
2. _____ 2. sometimes
3. _____ 3. outside
4. _____ 4. someone
5. _____ 5. anything
6. _____ 6. without
7. _____ 7. sidewalk
8. _____ 8. afternoon
9. _____ 9. playground
10. _____ 10. newspaper
11. _____ 11. notebook
12. _____ 12. basketball
13. _____ 13. barnyard
14. _____ 14. cardboard
15. _____ 15. fingernails

Challenge Words

_____ adult
_____ calm
_____ feast
_____ mammal
_____ swallow

Compound Words

Using the Word Study Steps

1. LOOK at the word.

2. SAY the word aloud.

3. STUDY the letters in the word.

4. WRITE the word.

5. CHECK the word.
   Did you spell the word right?
   If not, go back to step 1.

Compound Riddles

Join two words from the riddle to make up a compound word.

1. a ground where you play   _____

2. a barn on your yard   _____

3. the side where you walk   _____

4. a basket for the ball   _____

5. a book with a note   _____

6. the nails on your finger   _____

7. the side that's out   _____

8. the paper with news   _____

9. the thing for every need   _____

10. noon and then after   _____

McGraw-Hill School Division

Compound Words

everything	someone	sidewalk	newspaper	barnyard
sometimes	anything	afternoon	notebook	cardboard
outside	without	playground	basketball	fingernails

Look at the words in the box.
Write the spelling words with two syllables on the lines below.

1. _____ 2. _____ 3. _____

4. _____ 5. _____ 6. _____

7. _____ 8. _____ 9. _____

Write the spelling words with three syllables on the lines below.

10. _____ 11. _____ 12. _____

13. _____ 14. _____ 15. _____

What's in a Word?

Compound words are made up of smaller words. Write the spelling words
that have each of these words as part of it on the line.

16. some _____ _____

17. thing _____ _____

18. side _____ _____

19. book _____

Compound Words

everything	someone	sidewalk	newspaper	barnyard
sometimes	anything	afternoon	notebook	cardboard
outside	without	playground	basketball	fingernails

Write the spelling word to complete each sentence.

1. I haven't done _____ all day.

2. The cat takes a nap in the _____.

3. My sister's _____ are painted red.

4. I am on the school's _____ team.

5. Would you like _____ to go with you?

Definitions
Write the spelling word that matches the definition.

1. home for farm animals _____

2. material made of paper _____

3. free from _____ **4.** next to the street _____

Opposites
Write the spelling word that is the opposite in meaning to the word below.

inside   nothing   never

5. _____ **6.** _____ **7.** _____

Where Would It Be?
Write the spelling word that would most likely be found in each of these places:

next to a school   on a student's desk   in the library

8. _____ **9.** _____ **10.** _____

Challenge Extension: Imagine you went on a class trip to the circus, a museum, or an aquarium. Write sentences for each of the Challenge Words, describing what you might see.

118

Book 3.2/Unit 1
Big Blue Whale

15

Compound Words

Proofreading

There are six spelling mistakes in the paragraph below. Circle the misspelled words. Write the words correctly on the lines below.

    Last Saturday, our school held a fair in the school playgrond. Evrything at the fair was very exciting. Some children played baskitball while others drew on the sidewark with colored chalk. A bernyard was set up with a petting zoo. Children were invited to paint pictures of baby animals on cardbord to take home.

1. _____ 2. _____ 3. _____

4. _____ 5. _____ 6. _____

Writing Activity

Think about an interesting event that you have attended. Write a few sentences describing the event. Use four spelling words in your description.

_____

_____

_____

_____

Compound Words

Look at the words in each set. One word in each set is spelled correctly.
Use a pencil to color in the circle in front of that word. Before you begin,
look at the sample sets of words. Sample A has been done for you.
Do Sample B by yourself. When you are sure you know what to do,
you may go on with the rest of the page.

Sample A
- Ⓐ anyhowe
- Ⓑ innyhow
- Ⓒ ennyhow
- Ⓓ anyhow ●

Sample B
- Ⓔ cryed
- Ⓕ cried
- Ⓖ kried
- Ⓗ kryed

1.
- Ⓐ cardbored
- Ⓑ cardboard
- Ⓒ cardbord
- Ⓓ cardbird

2.
- Ⓔ bascetball
- Ⓕ baskitball
- Ⓖ baskatball
- Ⓗ basketball

3.
- Ⓐ noozpaper
- Ⓑ nuespaper
- Ⓒ newspaper
- Ⓓ noospaper

4.
- Ⓐ afternoon
- Ⓕ afternune
- Ⓖ afternoun
- Ⓗ afternown

5.
- Ⓐ without
- Ⓑ whithout
- Ⓒ wittout
- Ⓓ wethout

6.
- Ⓔ somewun
- Ⓕ someone
- Ⓖ sumwun
- Ⓗ sumone

7.
- Ⓐ sometimes
- Ⓑ sometymes
- Ⓒ sometimz
- Ⓓ suhmtimes

8.
- Ⓔ fingernailes
- Ⓕ fingernayles
- Ⓖ fingernails
- Ⓗ fingernales

9.
- Ⓐ barnyard
- Ⓑ bairnyard
- Ⓒ barnyerd
- Ⓓ barnyird

10.
- Ⓔ noatbook
- Ⓕ notebook
- Ⓖ notebuk
- Ⓗ nootbook

11.
- Ⓐ plaigrrund
- Ⓑ playegrownde
- Ⓒ playground
- Ⓓ playgrownd

12.
- Ⓔ sighedwalk
- Ⓕ sidewalk
- Ⓖ sidewerk
- Ⓗ sidewawk

13.
- Ⓐ evrything
- Ⓑ ehverything
- Ⓒ everything
- Ⓓ everrything

14.
- Ⓐ anything
- Ⓕ anytheeng
- Ⓖ ennything
- Ⓗ innything

15.
- Ⓐ owtside
- Ⓑ outside
- Ⓒ outsighed
- Ⓓ ootside

Words from Science

Pretest Directions

Fold back the paper along the dotted line. Use the blanks to write each word as it is read aloud. When you finish the test, unfold the paper. Use the list at the right to correct any spelling mistakes. Practice the words you missed for the Posttest.

To Parents

Here are the results of your child's weekly spelling Pretest. You can help your child study for the Posttest by following these simple steps for each word on the word list:

1. Read the word to your child.

2. Have your child write the word, saying each letter as it is written.

3. Say each letter of the word as your child checks the spelling.

4. If a mistake has been made, have your child read each letter of the correctly spelled word aloud, and then repeat steps 1-3.

1. _____	1. second
2. _____	2. mass
3. _____	3. week
4. _____	4. gram
5. _____	5. hour
6. _____	6. pounds
7. _____	7. scale
8. _____	8. month
9. _____	9. ounce
10. _____	10. data
11. _____	11. pint
12. _____	12. gallon
13. _____	13. problems
14. _____	14. meter
15. _____	15. measure

Challenge Words

_____	compared
_____	experts
_____	gain
_____	powdered
_____	switched

15 Book 3.2/Unit 1
J.J's Big Day

Words from Science

Using the Word Study Steps

1. LOOK at the word.

2. SAY the word aloud.

3. STUDY the letters in the word.

4. WRITE the word.

5. CHECK the word.
   Did you spell the word right?
   If not, go back to step 1.

X the word

Put an x on the word does not contain the small word in dark type.

1. **as**	mass	measure	scale
2. **pin**	pint	spin	point
3. **our**	sour	pounds	hour
4. **all**	gallon	scale	ball
5. **rob**	robber	problems	gram
6. **me**	meter	week	measure
7. **ram**	gram	grade	program
8. **at**	cat	data	meter
9. **on**	ounce	second	month
10. **we**	week	measure	well

Spelling Tip

• Think of times you may have seen the word in reading, on signs, or in a textbook. Try to remember how it looked. Write the word in different ways. Which one looks correct? secind, secund, second

• When words end in silent **e**, drop the **e** when adding an ending that begins with a vowel. When adding an ending that begins with a consonant, keep the silent **e**.

measure + ed = measu<u>red</u>

To Parents or Helpers:

Using the Word Study Steps above as your child comes across any new words will help him or her spell well. Review the steps as you both go over this week's spelling words.

Go over each Spelling Tip with your child. Help your child write words in different ways to see which one looks right. Help him or her find other words that end in silent **e** and drop the *e* when adding an ending that begins with a vowel.

Help your child find and circle the spelling words in the puzzle.

McGraw-Hill School Division

Words from Science

second	gram	scale	data	problems
mass	hour	month	pint	meter
week	pounds	ounce	gallon	measure

Pattern Power!

Write the spelling words with vowel sounds spelled with one letter.

1. _____ 2. _____ 3. _____

4. _____ 5. _____ 6. _____

7. _____ 8. _____ 9. _____

Write the spelling words with vowel sounds spelled with more than one letter.

10. _____ 11. _____ 12. _____

13. _____ 14. _____ 15. _____

Place the words from the box in alphabetical order.

16. _____ 17. _____ 18. _____

19. _____ 20. _____ 21. _____

22. _____ 23. _____ 24. _____

25. _____ 26. _____ 27. _____

28. _____ 29. _____ 30. _____

Words from Science

second	gram	scale	data	problems
mass	hour	month	pint	meter
week	pounds	ounce	gallon	measure

Finish the Sentence

Complete each sentence below using a spelling word.

1. There are 2000_____ in a ton.

2. A _____ is a just a little longer than a yard.

3. Put the package on the _____ and tell me how much it weighs.

4. Stand in front of the ruler so I can _____ your height.

5. January is the first _____ of the year.

6. There are two cups in a _____.

7. There are four quarts in a _____.

8. The place between first and third is _____.

9. A paper clip weighs about a _____.

10. In one pound, there are sixteen_____.

Definitions

Write the spelling word that matches the definition.

11. _____   seven days

12. _____   information

13. _____   sixty minutes

14. _____   questions to be answered

15. _____   weight

Challenge Extension: Have students create word-search puzzles that include all the Challenge Words. Then have students trade papers and solve each other's puzzles.

Book 3.2/Unit 1
J.J.'s Big Day 15

McGraw-Hill School Division

Words from Science

Proofreading

There are six spelling mistakes in the paragraph below. Circle the misspelled words. Write the words correctly on the lines below.

Today our class learned how to mesure all kinds of things. We learned that a weak is made up of seven days. To find out how many ponds something weighs, you can put it on a scayle. A grame is smaller than an once.

1. _____ 2. _____ 3. _____

4. _____ 5. _____ 6. _____

Writing Activity

People measure things all the time. Think about the kinds of things you might measure in a typical day. Then write a few sentences about how people use measurements in their everyday lives. Use four spelling words.

_____

_____

_____

_____

_____

Words from Science

Look at the words in each set. One word in each set is spelled correctly.
Use a pencil to color in the circle in front of that word. Before you begin,
look at the sample sets of words. Sample A has been done for you.
Do Sample B by yourself. When you are sure you know what to do,
you may go on with the rest of the page.

Sample A
- (A) howse
- (B) houz
- (C) house
- (D) huse

Sample B
- (E) funnie
- (F) funy
- (G) funny
- (H) funie

1.
- (A) weeke
- (B) weake
- (C) week
- (D) weke

2.
- (E) oure
- (F) houre
- (G) hoor
- (H) hour

3.
- (A) scayle
- (B) scale
- (C) skale
- (D) schale

4.
- (E) ounze
- (F) ownce
- (G) ounce
- (H) ounse

5.
- (A) pint
- (B) synt
- (C) pinte
- (D) pynte

6.
- (E) problums
- (F) problims
- (G) prablems
- (H) problems

7.
- (A) measure
- (B) mesure
- (C) meazure
- (D) mezure

8.
- (E) secund
- (F) sekund
- (G) second
- (H) secend

9.
- (A) meeter
- (B) meter
- (C) meetre
- (D) metere

10.
- (A) gallon
- (F) galon
- (G) gallun
- (H) gallin

11.
- (A) dadah
- (B) datta
- (C) dadda
- (D) data

12.
- (E) munth
- (F) month
- (G) munthe
- (H) moonth

13.
- (A) pondz
- (B) pouns
- (C) pounds
- (D) pownds

14.
- (A) gram
- (F) grame
- (G) graem
- (H) grem

15.
- (A) maz
- (B) mas
- (C) masse
- (D) mass

McGraw-Hill School Division

Book 3.2/Unit 1 Review Test

Read each sentence. If an underlined word is spelled wrong, fill in the circle that goes with that word. If no word is spelled wrong, fill in the circle below NONE.
Read Sample A, and do Sample B.

A. The <u>fish</u> <u>spesh</u> all day in the <u>river</u>.
        A   B   C

NONE

A. Ⓐ ● Ⓒ Ⓓ

B. The <u>snowflack</u> will <u>melt</u> in the <u>heat</u>.
        E   F   G

NONE

B. Ⓔ Ⓕ Ⓖ Ⓗ

1. The <u>fourth</u> one on <u>line</u> is a very tall <u>wuman</u>.
       A   B   C

NONE

1. Ⓐ Ⓑ Ⓒ Ⓓ

2. We <u>bought</u> <u>evrything</u> in an <u>afternoon</u>.
        E   F   G

NONE

2. Ⓔ Ⓕ Ⓖ Ⓗ

3. I had to <u>measure</u> how <u>thicke</u> the <u>whisker</u> was.
          A   B   C

NONE

3. Ⓐ Ⓑ Ⓒ Ⓓ

4. We get <u>thersty</u> when we <u>splash</u> in the <u>playground</u>.
        E   F   G

NONE

4. Ⓔ Ⓕ Ⓖ Ⓗ

5. I ate a <u>cherry</u> and a <u>peche</u>, <u>underneath</u> a tree.
       A   B   C

NONE

5. Ⓐ Ⓑ Ⓒ Ⓓ

6. This <u>monthe</u> we will meet one <u>hour</u> each <u>week</u>.
       E   F   G

NONE

6. Ⓔ Ⓕ Ⓖ Ⓗ

7. I want to <u>sketche</u> my <u>shadow</u> on the <u>sidewalk</u>.
         A   B   C

NONE

7. Ⓐ Ⓑ Ⓒ Ⓓ

8. I read a <u>newspaper</u> for an <u>houre</u> this <u>afternoon</u>.
         E   F   G

NONE

8. Ⓔ Ⓕ Ⓖ Ⓗ

9. Please pass a <u>seconde</u> <u>cookie</u> <u>across</u> the table.
          A   B   C

NONE

9. Ⓐ Ⓑ Ⓒ Ⓓ

10. I <u>bought</u> a <u>cookie</u> in the <u>playgruond</u>.
      E   F   G

NONE

10. Ⓔ Ⓕ Ⓖ Ⓗ

Go on

11. The <u>second</u> <u>shadowe</u> was of a <u>woman</u>.
        A   B   C

NONE
11. Ⓐ Ⓑ Ⓒ Ⓓ

12. Put the <u>peach</u> <u>underneath</u> the <u>cherrie</u> tree.
        E   F   G

NONE
12. Ⓔ Ⓕ Ⓖ Ⓗ

13. I <u>bought</u> a <u>newspaper</u> last <u>week</u>.
    A   B   C

NONE
13. Ⓐ Ⓑ Ⓒ Ⓓ

14. The <u>cookie</u> I <u>bought</u> was <u>thick.</u>
      E   F   G

NONE
14. Ⓔ Ⓕ Ⓖ Ⓗ

15. I want to <u>sketch</u> the <u>peach</u> tree <u>acros</u> the street.
          A   B   C

NONE
15. Ⓐ Ⓑ Ⓒ Ⓓ

16. I'll <u>measure</u> <u>across</u> the <u>sidewalk</u>.
      E   F   G

NONE
16. Ⓔ Ⓕ Ⓖ Ⓗ

17. Let's <u>splash</u> <u>everething</u> on the <u>newspaper</u>.
       A   B   C

NONE
17. Ⓐ Ⓑ Ⓒ Ⓓ

18. This is the first <u>weeke</u> of the <u>fourth</u> <u>month</u>.
             E   F G

NONE
18. Ⓔ Ⓕ Ⓖ Ⓗ

19. The cat has a <u>second</u> <u>thick</u> <u>wiscker</u>.
           A   B   C

NONE
19. Ⓐ Ⓑ Ⓒ Ⓓ

20. The <u>peach</u> fell <u>underneth</u> the <u>sidewalk</u>.
      E   F   G

NONE
20. Ⓔ Ⓕ Ⓖ Ⓗ

21. I was <u>born</u> in the <u>forth</u> <u>month.</u>
      A   B C

NONE
21. Ⓐ Ⓑ Ⓒ Ⓓ

22. We <u>found</u> the <u>neewspapir</u> on the <u>sidewalk</u>.
      E   F   G

NONE
22. Ⓔ Ⓕ Ⓖ Ⓗ

23. I can <u>meshure</u> the <u>sketch</u> <u>across</u> the top.
       A   B C

NONE
23. Ⓐ Ⓑ Ⓒ Ⓓ

24. At noon, my <u>shadow</u> is <u>thick</u> and not <u>tall.</u>
         E   F   G

NONE
24. Ⓔ Ⓕ Ⓖ Ⓗ

25. I <u>bought</u> a <u>cookie</u> in the <u>afternoone</u>.
    A   B   C

NONE
25. Ⓐ Ⓑ Ⓒ Ⓓ

McGraw-Hill School Division

Words with Soft *c* and Soft *g*

Pretest Directions

Fold back the paper along the dotted line. Use the blanks to write each word as it is read aloud. When you finish the test, unfold the paper. Use the list at the right to correct any spelling mistakes. Practice the words you missed for the Posttest.

To Parents

Here are the results of your child's weekly spelling Pretest. You can help your child study for the Posttest by following these simple steps for each word on the word list:

1. Read the word to your child.

2. Have your child write the word, saying each letter as it is written.

3. Say each letter of the word as your child checks the spelling.

4. If a mistake has been made, have your child read each letter of the correctly spelled word aloud, and then repeat steps 1-3.

1. _____ 1. sisters
2. _____ 2. giant
3. _____ 3. once
4. _____ 4. city
5. _____ 5. stage
6. _____ 6. jewels
7. _____ 7. judge
8. _____ 8. twice
9. _____ 9. message
10. _____ 10. circle
11. _____ 11. gym
12. _____ 12. rage
13. _____ 13. jolly
14. _____ 14. ledge
15. _____ 15. sunset

Challenge Words

_____ delighted
_____ disguised
_____ furious
_____ paced
_____ route

Words with Soft *c* and Soft *g*

Using the Word Study Steps

1. LOOK at the word.

2. SAY the word aloud.

3. STUDY the letters in the word.

4. WRITE the word.

5. CHECK the word.
   Did you spell the word right?
   If not, go back to step 1.

Spelling Tip

When the /s/ sound is spelled **c**, **c** is always followed by **e**, **i**, or **y**.
Examples:
   certain, circus, fancy

When /j/ is spelled **g**, **g** is always followed by **e**, **i**, or **y**.
Examples: page, giant, gym

Short vowels are followed by **dge**. Long vowels are followed by **ge**.
Examples:
   ju<u>dge</u>   sta<u>ge</u>

Riddles

Circle the spelling word that solves each riddle.

1. Why are Pam and Mary not brothers? (sisters, jewel, sunset)

2. When does the sun go down? (ledge, sunset, rage)

3. Who's bigger than big? (giant, jolly, twice)

4. What is another word for gem? (circle, jewel, ledge)

5. Who put the thief in jail?(sunset, once, judge)

6. What is round and not a square? (circle, sisters, city)

7. What do you get by phone or by mail? (jolly, sunset, message)

8. How happy is the fellow?(stage, jolly, rage)

9. Where can a bird perch? (giant, jewels, ledge)

10. What can a small town become? (sisters, city, circle)

To Parents or Helpers:
  Using the Word Study Steps above as your child comes across any new words will help him or her spell well. Review the steps as you both go over this week's spelling words.
  Go over each Spelling Tip with your child. Ask him or her to find and pronounce other new words that follow each of the rules in the Spelling Tips.
  Help your child find and circle the spelling words in the riddles.

McGraw-Hill School Division

Words with Soft *c* and Soft *g*

sisters	city	judge	circle	jolly
giant	stage	twice	gym	ledge
once	jewels	message	rage	sunset

Word Sort

Write the spelling words that have soft **c** spelled.

s

1. _____

2. _____

ce

3. _____

4. _____

c

5. _____

6. _____

ss

7. _____

Write the spelling words that have soft **g** spelled.

j

8. _____

9. _____

g

10. _____

11. _____

dge

12. _____

13. _____

ge

14. _____

15. _____

16. _____

How Do You Spell It?

How can you tell if a word that ends with the /j/ sound is spelled **ge** or **dge**? If a short vowel sound is followed by /j/, the /j/ is usually spelled **dge**, as in **edge**. If a long vowel sound is followed by /j/, it is usually spelled **ge**, as in **age**.

Circle the letter of the word in each pair that is correctly spelled

17. A stage
   B stadge

18. C lege
   D ledge

19. A radge
   B rage

20. C judge
   D juge

Words with Soft *c* and Soft *g*

sisters	city	judge	circle	jolly
giant	stage	twice	gym	ledge
once	jewels	message	rage	sunset

Fill in the Blanks

Complete each sentence below with a spelling word or words.

1. He left a _____ on the answering machine.

2. Grandmother visits _____ a week.

3. Stan has one brother and two _____.

4. The actors entered from the left side of the _____.

5. We went outside to watch the beautiful _____.

6. The country mouse didn't enjoy life in the big _____.

7. Although Michael appeared calm, he was filled with _____.

8. We like to play basketball in the _____.

9. The treasure chest was filled with _____.

10. We put our chairs in a _____ to play the game.

11. The _____ panda was even bigger than we expected.

12. Why do fairy tales always begin, "_____ upon a time"?

Write a sentence for each spelling word not used above. Circle the spelling word in each sentence.

_____

_____

_____

_____

Challenge Extension: Have students draw a picture to illustrate each challenge word. Then have students exchange their papers and see if they can identify the words illustrated by each other's drawings.

Book 3.2/Unit 2
Lon Po Po | 15

McGraw-Hill School Division

Words with Soft *c* and Soft *g*

Proofreading Activity

There are six spelling mistakes in this paragraph. Circle the misspelled words. Write the words correctly on the lines below.

Once upon a time, there were two sisters named Ella and Bella. One day, Ella decided to travel through the woods to the big citee to seek her fortune. "Beware the horrible giant who lives in the woods," said Bella, but Ella refused to listen to her mesage. When she reached the woods, she met a man who was twise as tall as the tallest tree in the forest. Ella was scared, but the huge man was quite joly and not filled with rage at all. Instead of harming the frightened girl, the huge man gave her a bag full of precious jools! Ella returned home and shared her fortune with Bella. The two girls agreed that they would never again juge people by the way they look.

1. _____ 2. _____ 3. _____

4. _____ 5. _____ 6. _____

Writing Activity

Things are very often not as they seem. Have you ever been surprised when someone or something turned out to be quite different from what you expected? Write a few sentences describing that experience. If you prefer, you can make up a story about someone or something that turns out not to be what it seems. Use four spelling words.

_____

_____

_____

_____

_____

Words with Soft *c* and Soft *g*

Look at the words in each set. One word in each set is spelled correctly.
Use a pencil to color in the circle in front of that word. Before you begin,
look at the sample sets of words. Sample A has been done for you.
Do Sample B by yourself. When you are sure you know what to do,
you may go on with the rest of the page.

Sample A
(A) witt
(B) wo
(C) with
(D) withe

Sample B
(E) techer
(F) techur
(G) teecher
(H) teacher

1. (A) gient
   (B) jiant
   (C) giant
   (D) giante

2. (E) citee
   (F) city
   (G) sity
   (H) citie

3. (A) jools
   (B) jewls
   (C) jewels
   (D) jewels

4. (E) twice
   (F) twict
   (G) twise
   (H) twyse

5. (A) cyrcle
   (B) circle
   (C) sircle
   (D) circal

6. (E) raje
   (F) rayge
   (G) rayj
   (H) rage

7. (A) ledge
   (B) lege
   (C) leje
   (D) ledje

8. (E) sunsett
   (F) sunset
   (G) sunsette
   (H) sonset

9. (A) joly
   (B) jollie
   (C) jolly
   (D) jolie

10. (E) gym
    (F) gim
    (G) jym
    (H) jim

11. (A) mesage
    (B) message
    (C) mesagge
    (D) massege

12. (E) judg
    (F) judje
    (G) juge
    (H) judge

13. (A) stage
    (B) stadge
    (C) stayge
    (D) staje

14. (E) wunce
    (F) wonce
    (G) once
    (H) wunse

15. (A) sistas
    (B) sistres
    (C) sisters
    (D) scisters

McGraw-Hill School Division

Words with /är/ and /ûr/

Pretest Directions

Fold back the paper along the dotted line. Use the blanks to write each word as it is read aloud. When you finish the test, unfold the paper. Use the list at the right to correct any spelling mistakes. Practice the words you missed for the Posttest.

To Parents

Here are the results of your child's weekly spelling Pretest. You can help your child study for the Posttest by following these simple steps for each word on the word list:

1. Read the word to your child.

2. Have your child write the word, saying each letter as it is written.

3. Say each letter of the word as your child checks the spelling.

4. If a mistake has been made, have your child read each letter of the correctly spelled word aloud, and then repeat steps 1-3.

#		#	Word
1.	_____	1.	turtle
2.	_____	2.	words
3.	_____	3.	sharp
4.	_____	4.	learn
5.	_____	5.	person
6.	_____	6.	firm
7.	_____	7.	market
8.	_____	8.	worth
9.	_____	9.	skirt
10.	_____	10.	search
11.	_____	11.	merchant
12.	_____	12.	alarm
13.	_____	13.	world
14.	_____	14.	curtain
15.	_____	15.	startle

Challenge Words

_____ attack

_____ bother

_____ expects

_____ label

_____ temperature

McGraw-Hill School Division

Words with /är/ and /ûr/

Using the Word Study Steps

1. LOOK at the word.

2. SAY the word aloud.

3. STUDY the letters in the word.

4. WRITE the word.

5. CHECK the word.
   Did you spell the word right?
   If not, go back to step 1.

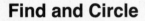

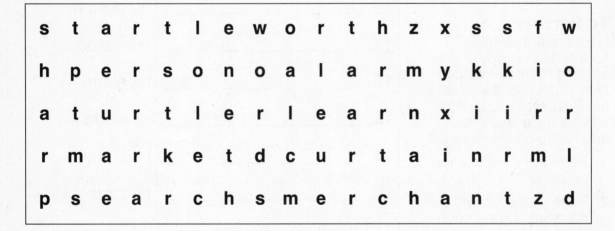

Spelling Tip

Think of times you may have seen a word in reading, on signs, or in a textbook. Try to remember how it looked. Write the word in different ways. Which one looks correct?
Example:
~~havy,~~ ~~hevy,~~ heavy

Find and Circle

Where are the spelling words?

```
s  t  a  r  t  l  e  w  o  r  t  h  z  x  s  s  f  w
h  p  e  r  s  o  n  o  a  l  a  r  m  y  k  k  i  o
a  t  u  r  t  l  e  r  l  e  a  r  n  x  i  i  r  r
r  m  a  r  k  e  t  d  c  u  r  t  a  i  n  r  m  l
p  s  e  a  r  c  h  s  m  e  r  c  h  a  n  t  z  d
```

To Parents or Helpers:
    Using the Word Study Steps above as your child comes across any new words will help him or her spell well. Review the steps as you both go over this week's spelling words.
    Go over the Spelling Tip with your child. Help your child write words in different ways to see which one looks right. Also help your child write words that they have trouble spelling in a notebook that they can keep.
    Help your child find and circle the spelling words in the puzzle.

Words with /är/ and /ûr/

Pattern Power!

This week's spelling words contain the vowel sounds /är/ and /ûr/. Write each spelling word under the word that has the same vowel sound.

part

1. _____   3. _____

2. _____   4. _____

shirt

5. _____   9. _____   13. _____

6. _____   10. _____   14. _____

7. _____   11. _____   15. _____

8. _____   12. _____

Write the spelling words that have these patterns:

/ûr/ spelled *ur*	/ûr/ spelled *or*	/ûr/ spelled *ir*
16. _____	18. _____	21. _____
17. _____	19. _____	22. _____
	20. _____	

/ûr/ spelled *er*	/ûr/ spelled *ear*	/är/ spelled *ar*
23. _____	25. _____	27. _____
24. _____	26. _____	28. _____
		29. _____
		30. _____

Words with /är/ and /ûr/

Synonym Alert!

Write the spelling words that have the same meanings as the words below.

1. pointed   _____

2. surprise   _____

3. seek   _____

4. unmoved   _____

What's the Word?

Complete each sentence with a spelling word.

5. When you go to the _____, bring back some milk.

6. Did you remember to look up those _____ in the dictionary?

7. Most countries in the _____ belong to the United Nations.

8. A red shirt would go well with that _____.

9. You can close the _____ if it gets too bright.

10. The _____ hid its head inside its shell.

11. My _____ goes off every morning at seven o'clock.

12. He's not the kind of _____ who would lie to his friends.

13. Every _____ in town will be taking part in the special sale.

14. Someday I hope to _____ how to play the guitar.

15. This coin is so rare that it's _____ a lot of money.

Challenge Extension: Have students write a paragraph about an animal they know well.

Book 3.2/Unit 2
Animal Fact/Animal Fable 15

McGraw-Hill School Division

Words with /är/ and /ûr/

Proofreading Activity

There are six spelling mistakes in this report. Circle the misspelled words. Write the words correctly on the lines below.

I can hardly describe in wurdz how much fun we had last Saturday. There were many wonderful things for sale at the markit. You could find anything you wanted if you were willing to search for it. A merchant named Mr. Martin had a big tertle on his table. He kept it behind a curtain so it wouldn't startel anyone. "How much is it worth?" one persin asked. "Myrtle is my pet," Mr. Martin said. "I wouldn't sell her for all the money in the wurld!"

1. _____   2. _____   3. _____

4. _____   5. _____   6. _____

Writing Activity

Do you have any pets? If not, is there a pet you would like to have? Write a paragraph about a pet you have or wish you had. Use at least four words with the /är/ or /ûr/ sounds.

_____

_____

_____

_____

_____

Words with /är/ and /ûr/

Look at the words in each set. One word in each set is spelled correctly.
Use a pencil to color in the circle in front of that word. Before you begin,
look at the sample sets of words. Sample A has been done for you.
Do Sample B by yourself. When you are sure you know what to do,
you may go on with the rest of the page.

Sample A
- Ⓐ shork
- Ⓑ sherk
- ⬤ shark
- Ⓓ shurk

Sample B
- Ⓔ furst
- Ⓕ farst
- Ⓖ ferst
- Ⓗ first

1.
- Ⓐ startel
- Ⓑ startal
- Ⓒ startle
- Ⓓ startil

2.
- Ⓔ wurld
- Ⓕ world
- Ⓖ whirld
- Ⓗ werld

3.
- Ⓐ merchant
- Ⓑ merchent
- Ⓒ mercant
- Ⓓ marchant

4.
- Ⓔ skert
- Ⓕ skirt
- Ⓖ skeert
- Ⓗ skirte

5.
- Ⓐ marchet
- Ⓑ markette
- Ⓒ mercket
- Ⓓ market

6.
- Ⓔ personne
- Ⓕ perrson
- Ⓖ person
- Ⓗ persen

7.
- Ⓐ sharp
- Ⓑ sharrp
- Ⓒ sharpe
- Ⓓ scharp

8.
- Ⓔ tertle
- Ⓕ turtel
- Ⓖ tertel
- Ⓗ turtle

9.
- Ⓐ curtian
- Ⓑ curtain
- Ⓒ curtin
- Ⓓ curtan

10.
- Ⓔ alerm
- Ⓕ alarm
- Ⓖ alam
- Ⓗ alarme

11.
- Ⓐ search
- Ⓑ serch
- Ⓒ saerch
- Ⓓ serche

12.
- Ⓔ wurth
- Ⓕ wirth
- Ⓖ wourth
- Ⓗ worth

13.
- Ⓐ ferm
- Ⓑ furm
- Ⓒ firm
- Ⓓ furme

14.
- Ⓔ lurn
- Ⓕ lern
- Ⓖ learn
- Ⓗ lurne

15.
- Ⓐ words
- Ⓑ wurds
- Ⓒ wourds
- Ⓓ wirds

Words with /âr/, /ôr/, /îr/

Pretest Directions

Fold back the paper along the dotted line. Use the blanks to write each word as it is read aloud. When you finish the test, unfold the paper. Use the list at the right to correct any spelling mistakes. Practice the words you missed for the Posttest.

To Parents

Here are the results of your child's weekly spelling Pretest. You can help your child study for the Posttest by following these simple steps for each word on the word list:

1. Read the word to your child.

2. Have your child write the word, saying each letter as it is written.

3. Say each letter of the word as your child checks the spelling.

4. If a mistake has been made, have your child read each letter of the correctly spelled word aloud, and then repeat steps 1-3.

1. _____	1. store
2. _____	2. near
3. _____	3. fair
4. _____	4. storm
5. _____	5. stare
6. _____	6. deer
7. _____	7. hair
8. _____	8. beard
9. _____	9. glare
10. _____	10. important
11. _____	11. engineer
12. _____	12. sore
13. _____	13. dare
14. _____	14. force
15. _____	15. weary

Challenge Words

_____ advice

_____ curious

_____ discuss

_____ experiment

_____ scientific

Words with /âr/, /ôr/, /îr/

Using the Word Study Steps

1. LOOK at the word.

2. SAY the word aloud.

3. STUDY the letters in the word.

4. WRITE the word.

5. CHECK the word.
   Did you spell the word right?
   If not, go back to step 1.

Spelling Tip

Think of a word you know, such as a rhyming word, that has the same spelling pattern as the word you want to spell.
Examples:

care, dare, stare

X the word

Put an x on the word does not contain the small word in dark type.

1.	**are**	dare	stare	chair
2.	**air**	glare	hair	fair
3.	**or**	storm	deer	important
4.	**ear**	weary	engineer	beard
5.	**for**	force	before	store
6.	**ore**	sore	store	force
7.	**air**	stair	pair	care
8.	**ort**	port	share	sort
9.	**for**	torn	fort	enforce
10.	**ear**	tear	near	here

To Parents or Helpers:
    Using the Word Study Steps above as your child comes across any new words will help him or her spell well. Review the steps as you both go over this week's spelling words.
    Go over the Spelling Tip with your child. Help your child think of other rhyming words that have the same spelling pattern.
    Help your child find and circle the spelling words in the puzzle.

Words with /âr/, /ôr/, /îr/

Pattern Power!

Write the spelling words for each spelling pattern.

are

1. _____

2. _____

3. _____

air

4. _____

5. _____

or

6. _____

7. _____

8. _____

9. _____

10. _____

ear

11. _____

12. _____

13. _____

eer

14. _____

15. _____

Rhyme Time

Write the spelling words that rhyme with the words below.

16. teary _____

17. warm _____

18. course _____

19. core _____

Words with /âr/, /ôr/, /îr/

Analogies

An analogy is a statement that compares sets of words that are alike in some way: **night** is to **day** as **black** is to **white**. This analogy points out that **night** and **day** are opposite in the same way that **black** and **white** are opposite.

Use spelling words to complete the analogies below.

1. **On** is to **off** as **far** is to _____.

2. **Small** is to **little** as **tired** is to _____.

3. **Car** is to **driver** as **train** is to _____.

4. **Desert** is to **camel** as **forest** is to _____.

Definition, Please!

Write the spelling word that matches each definition.

5. Foul weather _____

6. Natural head covering _____

7. Place where goods are kept or sold _____

8. Challenge _____

9. Make someone do something _____

10. Painful _____

Challenge Extension: Have students scramble the letters in each challenge word. Then have students exchange their scrambled words with a partner to be solved.

144

Book 3.2/Unit 2
The Many Lives of Benjamin Franklin
10

McGraw-Hill School Division

Words with /âr/, /ôr/, /îr/

Proofreading Activity

There are six spelling mistakes in this group of statements. Circle the misspelled words. Write the words correctly on the lines below.

Ideas About Interesting Jobs

1. Someday, I would like to be an enginear.
2. My father has a very importent job.
3 He is a detective on the city police forse.
4. If I worked at the nature center, I would be neer birds, deer, and raccoons.
5. I would like to work outdoors, but I wouldn't want to work during a sturme.
6. I would enjoy working in a fine furniture stor and selling tables and chairs.

1. _____   2. _____   3. _____

4. _____   5. _____   6. _____

Writing Activity

Have you ever thought about the kind of job you might like to have when you're grown up? Write four sentences about a job that seems interesting to you. Use four spelling words in your writing.

_____

_____

_____

_____

Words with /âr/, /ôr/, /îr/

Look at the words in each set. One word in each set is spelled correctly.
Use a pencil to color in the circle in front of that word. Before you begin,
look at the sample sets of words. Sample A has been done for you.
Do Sample B by yourself. When you are sure you know what to do,
you may go on with the rest of the page.

Sample A
(A) feer
(B) fere
(C) faer
(D) fear

Sample B
(E) blok
(F) blokc
(G) block
(H) blook

1. (A) nir
   (B) near
   (C) neer
   (D) ner

2. (E) storm
   (F) storme
   (G) stirm
   (H) sturm

3. (A) deere
   (B) dir
   (C) deer
   (D) dar

4. (E) burd
   (F) beard
   (G) bord
   (H) baerd

5. (A) emportant
   (B) importent
   (C) important
   (D) impertent

6. (E) sawr
   (F) sor
   (G) sar
   (H) sore

7. (A) force
   (B) firce
   (C) forse
   (D) fors

8. (E) stoar
   (F) store
   (G) stire
   (H) stahr

9. (A) fahr
   (B) fehr
   (C) fair
   (D) faire

10. (E) stehr
    (F) stere
    (G) stear
    (H) stare

11. (A) haire
    (B) hair
    (C) har
    (D) hahr

12. (E) glare
    (F) glair
    (G) glar
    (H) glear

13. (D) enginir
    (B) enginear
    (C) ingineer
    (D) engineer

14. (E) dare
    (F) dar
    (G) dahr
    (H) dore

15. (A) weery
    (B) weary
    (C) wirey
    (D) wairy

Contractions

Pretest Directions

Fold back the paper along the dotted line. Use the blanks to write each word as it is read aloud. When you finish the test, unfold the paper. Use the list at the right to correct any spelling mistakes. Practice the words you missed for the Posttest.

To Parents

Here are the results of your child's weekly spelling Pretest. You can help your child study for the Posttest by following these simple steps for each word on the word list:

1. Read the word to your child.

2. Have your child write the word, saying each letter as it is written.

3. Say each letter of the word as your child checks the spelling.

4. If a mistake has been made, have your child read each letter of the correctly spelled word aloud, and then repeat steps 1-3.

1. _____ 1. won't
2. _____ 2. you're
3. _____ 3. I'll
4. _____ 4. we've
5. _____ 5. it's
6. _____ 6. didn't
7. _____ 7. I'm
8. _____ 8. we're
9. _____ 9. don't
10. _____ 10. you'll
11. _____ 11. he's
12. _____ 12. doesn't
13. _____ 13. she'll
14. _____ 14. they've
15. _____ 15. shouldn't

Challenge Words

_____ avoid
_____ brief
_____ frequently
_____ gradual
_____ periods

Contractions

Using the Word Study Steps

1. LOOK at the word.

2. SAY the word aloud.

3. STUDY the letters in the word.

4. WRITE the word.

5. CHECK the word.
   Did you spell the word right?
   If not, go back to step 1.

Spelling Tip

An apostrophe (') takes the place of the letters that are left out.
Examples:
   I'm, he's, she's

Circle the Word

Circle the contraction that fits each sentence.

1. Sam (didn't, I'll, we've) go to school today.

2. (Doesn't, He's, Shouldn't) not feeling well.

3. He (shouldn't, we're, we've) have played in the rain.

4. I (won't, don't, doesn't) think he will go tomorrow

5. (It's, Won't, We're) going to make him a get well card.

6. (You'll, She'll, I'm) going to take it to Sam.

7. I think (they've, shouldn't, he'll) like it very much.

8. When you meet Sam, (you'll, it's, he's) like him a lot.

To Parents or Helpers:

Using the Word Study Steps above as your child comes across any new words will help him or her spell well. Review the steps as you both go over this week's spelling words.

Go over each Spelling Tip with your child. Help your child think of other contractions. Ask him or her to tell you which letters were taken out and replaced with an apostrophe.

Help your child find and circle the spelling words in the puzzle.

Contractions

Pattern Power!

Write the contractions that are made with each word below.

not

1. _____ 2. _____ 3. _____

4. _____ 5. _____

are

6. _____ 7. _____

have

8. _____ 9. _____

is

10. _____ 11. _____

will

12. _____ 13. _____ 14. _____

am

15. _____

Write the words that form the contractions below.

Example: she'll = she will

16. they've _____ **17.** you're _____

18. it's _____ **19.** doesn't _____

20. I'm _____

Contractions

Circle the Words

Circle the word in the parentheses that correctly completes the sentence.

1. We (won't, weren't) be going away this summer.

2. (He'll, He's) going to get in trouble with the teacher.

3. You (should've, shouldn't) start something you can't finish.

4. I (don't, doesn't) want to play that game anymore.

5. Do you know what (your, you're) going to wear to the party?

6. (Don't, Didn't) anyone tell you where to go?

7. (We've, We're) decided to meet at Clara's house.

8. Jamie said (she'll, she's) come if she's not too busy.

9. (I've, I'm) not sure what page the homework is on.

10. (It's, Its) almost time to leave.

Make a Sentence

Use each word in a sentence.

11. they've _____

12. I'll _____

13. we're _____

14. doesn't _____

15. you'll _____

Challenge Extension: Have students make a word-search puzzle that contains all the challenge words. Have each student exchange their puzzles with a partner and find the challenge words.

150

Book 3.2/Unit 2
Cloudy With a Chance of Meatballs | 15 |

McGraw-Hill School Division

Contractions

Proofreading Activity

There are six spelling mistakes in this letter. Circle the misspelled words. Write the words correctly on the lines below.

Dear Roger,

    You wo'nt believe what a great time we had on our trip to New York. Its amazing how many things there are to do there! Theyv'e got so many theaters and museums, you feel as if youl'l never have enough time to see it all. We dint even have a chance to see the United Nations or the Empire State Building. Im hoping we'll go back again sometime. I can hardly wait!

                          Your friend,

                          Arthur

1. _____ 2. _____ 3. _____

4. _____ 5. _____ 6. _____

Writing Activity

Write a letter to a friend. Describe an interesting place that you've visited or someplace you would like to visit. Use at least four contractions.

_____

_____

_____

_____

_____

Contractions

Look at the words in each set. One word in each set is spelled correctly.
Use a pencil to color in the circle in front of that word. Before you begin,
look at the sample sets of words. Sample A has been done for you.
Do Sample B by yourself. When you are sure you know what to do,
you may go on with the rest of the page.

Sample A
- Ⓐ thats
- ⬤Ⓑ that's
- Ⓒ thatz
- Ⓓ thats'

Sample B
- Ⓔ w'ed
- Ⓕ we'ed
- Ⓖ we'd
- Ⓗ wee'd

1.
- Ⓐ youre
- Ⓑ yo'ur
- Ⓒ you're
- Ⓓ yo're

2.
- Ⓔ wea've
- Ⓕ we've
- Ⓖ wev'e
- Ⓗ weve

3.
- Ⓐ din't
- Ⓑ didnt
- Ⓒ didn't
- Ⓓ did'nt

4.
- Ⓔ were'
- Ⓕ w'ere
- Ⓖ we're
- Ⓗ wer'e

5.
- Ⓐ your
- Ⓑ yo'll
- Ⓒ you'll
- Ⓓ youll

6.
- Ⓔ does'nt
- Ⓕ doesnt
- Ⓖ dosn't
- Ⓗ doesn't

7.
- Ⓐ theyve'
- Ⓑ the'vye
- Ⓒ they've
- Ⓓ theyve

8.
- Ⓔ won't
- Ⓕ wont'
- Ⓖ wo'nt
- Ⓗ wont

9.
- Ⓐ 'Ill
- Ⓑ Il'I
- Ⓒ Ill
- Ⓓ I'll

10.
- Ⓔ do'nt
- Ⓕ dont'
- Ⓖ don't
- Ⓗ dont

11.
- Ⓐ i'ts
- Ⓑ it's
- Ⓒ its
- Ⓓ itz

12.
- Ⓔ he'es
- Ⓕ hes'
- Ⓖ he's
- Ⓗ hes

13.
- Ⓐ 'Im
- Ⓑ I'm
- Ⓒ Im'
- Ⓓ 'm

14.
- Ⓔ sh el'l
- Ⓕ she ll'
- Ⓖ she'll
- Ⓗ shell

15.
- Ⓐ shouldnt
- Ⓑ shouldnt'
- Ⓒ shoudn't
- Ⓓ shouldn't

Words from Social Studies

Pretest Directions

Fold back the paper along the dotted line. Use the blanks to write each word as it is read aloud. When you finish the test, unfold the paper. Use the list at the right to correct any spelling mistakes. Practice the words you missed for the Posttest.

To Parents

Here are the results of your child's weekly spelling Pretest. You can help your child study for the Posttest by following these simple steps for each word on the word list:

1. Read the word to your child.

2. Have your child write the word, saying each letter as it is written.

3. Say each letter of the word as your child checks the spelling.

4. If a mistake has been made, have your child read each letter of the correctly spelled word aloud, and then repeat steps 1-3.

1. _____	1. coal
2. _____	2. sunlight
3. _____	3. globe
4. _____	4. gas
5. _____	5. save
6. _____	6. millions
7. _____	7. solar
8. _____	8. lumber
9. _____	9. climate
10. _____	10. planet
11. _____	11. recycle
12. _____	12. fossil
13. _____	13. windmills
14. _____	14. fuels
15. _____	15. natural

Challenge Words

_____ energy

_____ entire

_____ future

_____ model

_____ pollution

Words from Social Studies

Using the Word Study Steps

1. LOOK at the word.

2. SAY the word aloud.

3. STUDY the letters in the word.

4. WRITE the word.

5. CHECK the word.
   Did you spell the word right?
   If not, go back to step 1.

Spelling Tip

Learn to spell prefixes and suffixes you use often in writing.

Example:

recycle

Look for chunks or smaller words that help you remember the spelling of a word.

Example:

sun + light = sunlight

Find and Circle

Where are the spelling words?

```
w r e c y c l e g i s m m i l l i o n s f
g g l o b e a e g f o s s i l a s n a a u
a m n a t u r a l d l u m b e r q u v v e
s u n l i g h t o a a w p l a n e t e e l
q u c l i m a t e g r w i n d m i l l s s
```

To Parents or Helpers:

Using the Word Study Steps above as your child comes across any new words will help him or her spell well. Review the steps as you both go over this week's spelling words.

Go over each Spelling Tip with your child. Ask if he or she knows words with other prefixes that often are used in writing. Help him or her find helpful chunks or smaller words in other new words.

Help your child find and circle the spelling words in the puzzle.

Words from Social Studies

Pattern Power!

Write the spelling words that have the kinds of vowel sounds listed below. For words with more than one syllable, listen for the vowel sound in the first syllable.

short *a*

1. _____

2. _____

3. _____

short *o*

6. _____

short *a*

9. _____

long *i*

11. _____

long *u*

15. _____

short *i*

4. _____

5. _____

short *u*

7. _____

8. _____

long *e*

10. _____

long *o*

12. _____

13. _____

14. _____

Syllable Patterns

If the first syllable has a short vowel sound, usually divide after the consonant or between two consonants. If the first syllable has a long vowel sound, usually divide after the vowel.

Divide the spelling words into syllables.

16. lumber _____ **17.** solar _____

18. planet _____ **19.** fossil _____

20. climate _____

Words from Social Studies

What Does It Mean?

Write the spelling word that matches each clue below.

1. Getting power from the sun _____

2. Plant or animal remains found in rock _____

3. A model of the earth _____

4. Mars or Jupiter, for example _____

5. Used to build houses _____

6. A soft black rock _____

7. Temperature and rainfall are parts of it _____

8. Stop from being destroyed _____

9. Thousands of thousands _____

10. They turn breezes into energy _____

Prefixes

A prefix is a word part that appears at the beginning of a word and changes the meaning of the word. The prefix **re-** means "again." The prefix **un-** means "not." Use these two prefixes to form new words below.

11. un + natural = _____

12. re + heat = _____

13. un + clear = _____

14. re + cycle = _____

15. un + kind = _____

Challenge Extension: Have students write a sentence for each challenge word.

Book 3.2/Unit 2
Pure Power 15

McGraw-Hill School Division

Words from Social Studies

Proofreading Activity

There are six spelling mistakes in this article. Circle the misspelled words. Write the words correctly on the lines below.

   All of us must work together to sayve our planet. Each year, milions of trees are cut down to be used as lumber. Instead of burning cole and other fossil fuels, people can begin to use sunlite and wind as sources of energy. For example, we can use windmills to make electricity and soler energy to heat our houses. If we all remember to recykle, the world will be a cleaner and more beautiful home for us all.

1. _____   2. _____   3. _____

4. _____   5. _____   6. _____

Writing Activity

Suppose everyone suddenly stopped trying to save the earth's natural resources. Imagine a future in which all the forests have been cut down. Suppose we no longer have any oil or coal to use for energy. Write a short story about what life might be like in such a world. Use at least four spelling words in your story.

_____

_____

_____

_____

_____

Words from Social Studies

Look at the words in each set. One word in each set is spelled correctly.
Use a pencil to color in the circle in front of that word. Before you begin,
look at the sample sets of words. Sample A has been done for you.
Do Sample B by yourself. When you are sure you know what to do,
you may go on with the rest of the page.

Sample A
Ⓐ farmer
Ⓑ fahmer
Ⓒ farmar
Ⓓ farmir

Sample B
Ⓔ forist
Ⓕ farest
Ⓖ forest
Ⓗ forust

1. Ⓐ sunlite
   Ⓑ sonlight
   Ⓒ sunligth
   Ⓓ sunlight

2. Ⓔ gasse
   Ⓕ gas
   Ⓖ gaz
   Ⓗ gass

3. Ⓐ milions
   Ⓑ milyins
   Ⓒ millions
   Ⓓ mellions

4. Ⓔ lumber
   Ⓕ lumba
   Ⓖ lummber
   Ⓗ lumbe

5. Ⓐ plante
   Ⓑ planet
   Ⓒ plannet
   Ⓓ planete

6. Ⓔ fossle
   Ⓕ fossel
   Ⓖ fossal
   Ⓗ fossil

7. Ⓐ fuels
   Ⓑ fules
   Ⓒ fyools
   Ⓓ fuels

8. Ⓔ natchrel
   Ⓕ naturel
   Ⓖ natural
   Ⓗ nacheral

9. Ⓐ windmils
   Ⓑ windmills
   Ⓒ windmiles
   Ⓓ windmilles

10. Ⓔ recicle
    Ⓕ ricycle
    Ⓖ resycle
    Ⓗ recycle

11. Ⓐ climate
    Ⓑ climit
    Ⓒ climet
    Ⓓ clymate

12. Ⓔ sowler
    Ⓕ salor
    Ⓖ solar
    Ⓗ soler

13. Ⓐ save
    Ⓑ sayve
    Ⓒ seve
    Ⓓ sav

14. Ⓔ globe
    Ⓕ glowb
    Ⓖ galobe
    Ⓗ glowbe

15. Ⓐ cowle
    Ⓑ coal
    Ⓒ cole
    Ⓓ coel

McGraw-Hill School Division

Book 3.2/Unit 2 Review Test

Read each sentence. If an underlined word is spelled wrong, fill in the circle that goes with that word. If no word is spelled wrong, fill in the circle below NONE. Read Sample A, and do Sample B.

A. We saw a <u>giant</u> <u>oak</u> <u>tree</u>.
          A   B C
                         NONE
A. Ⓐ   Ⓑ   Ⓒ   ⬤

B. I <u>bought</u> a <u>pech</u> in the <u>afternoon</u>.
     E   F   G
                         NONE
B. Ⓔ   Ⓕ   Ⓖ   Ⓗ

1. The boat was in a <u>giant</u> <u>sturm</u> at <u>sunset</u>.
                A   B   C
                         NONE
1. Ⓐ   Ⓑ   Ⓒ   Ⓓ

2. He <u>wonte</u> <u>dare</u> grow a <u>beard</u>.
       E   F   G
                         NONE
2. Ⓔ   Ⓕ   Ⓖ   Ⓗ

3. We <u>lerne</u> about <u>sunlight</u> and <u>climate</u> in school.
    A   B   C
                         NONE
3. Ⓐ   Ⓑ   Ⓒ   Ⓓ

4. It seems as if a <u>citty</u> has <u>millions</u> of <u>buildings</u>.
                 E   F   G
                         NONE
4. Ⓔ   Ⓕ   Ⓖ   Ⓗ

5. <u>I'im</u> going to be an <u>engineer</u> or a <u>judge</u>.
    A   B   C
                         NONE
5. Ⓐ   Ⓑ   Ⓒ   Ⓓ

6. I <u>brush</u> my <u>hare</u> and comb my <u>beard</u>.
    E   F   G
                         NONE
6. Ⓔ   Ⓕ   Ⓖ   Ⓗ

7. <u>Weve</u> got to <u>recycle</u> the old <u>lumber</u>.
    A   B   C
                         NONE
7. Ⓐ   Ⓑ   Ⓒ   Ⓓ

8. <u>Milyons</u> of <u>people</u> live in the <u>city</u>.
    E   F   G
                         NONE
8. Ⓔ   Ⓕ   Ⓖ   Ⓗ

9. <u>He's</u> a <u>sharp</u> <u>judge</u> of horses.
    A   B   C
                         NONE
9. Ⓐ   Ⓑ   Ⓒ   Ⓓ

10. We <u>won't</u> take that <u>dear</u> <u>twice</u>.
     E   F G
                         NONE
10. Ⓔ   Ⓕ   Ⓖ   Ⓗ

Go on

11. <u>Ime</u> <u>always</u> looking for <u>lumber</u>.
   A   B   C

NONE
11. Ⓐ Ⓑ Ⓒ Ⓓ

12. The <u>engineer</u> has a <u>giant</u> black <u>beerd</u>.
       E   F   G

NONE
12. Ⓔ Ⓕ Ⓖ Ⓗ

13. You need <u>lumburr</u> to <u>build</u> a <u>city</u>.
          A   B   C

NONE
13. Ⓐ Ⓑ Ⓒ Ⓓ

14. We went up the <u>ladder</u> <u>twyse</u> to fix the <u>curtain</u>.
              E   F   G

NONE
14. Ⓔ Ⓕ Ⓖ Ⓗ

15. The <u>sonsett</u> made <u>everything</u> red and <u>gold</u>.
      A   B   C

NONE
15. Ⓐ Ⓑ Ⓒ Ⓓ

16. She <u>wore</u> a <u>skurtt</u> that was <u>worth</u> a lot of money.
     E   F   G

NONE
16. Ⓔ Ⓕ Ⓖ Ⓗ

17. <u>Call</u> the <u>inginere</u> to fix the <u>heat</u>.
   A   B   C

NONE
17. Ⓐ Ⓑ Ⓒ Ⓓ

18. <u>Yul</u> <u>sew</u> a <u>skert</u> in school.
   E   F   G

NONE
18. Ⓔ Ⓕ Ⓖ Ⓗ

19. They live in a <u>dry</u>, <u>warm</u> <u>clymit</u>.
          A   B   C

NONE
19. Ⓐ Ⓑ Ⓒ Ⓓ

20. The <u>giant</u> <u>sturm</u> flooded the <u>city</u>.
      E   F   G

NONE
20. Ⓔ Ⓕ Ⓖ Ⓗ

21. He will <u>dayre</u> to <u>learn</u> <u>everything</u>.
        A   B   C

NONE
21. Ⓐ Ⓑ Ⓒ Ⓓ

22. <u>Hes</u> <u>twice</u> as <u>sharp</u> as his brother.
   E   F   G

NONE
22. Ⓔ Ⓕ Ⓖ Ⓗ

23. Our <u>city</u> will <u>resykle</u> <u>newspapers</u>.
     A   B   C

NONE
23. Ⓐ Ⓑ Ⓒ Ⓓ

24. There is a <u>jyant</u> with a <u>beard</u> behind the <u>curtain</u>.
          E   F   G

NONE
24. Ⓔ Ⓕ Ⓖ Ⓗ

25. The <u>tree</u> had <u>sharpe</u> <u>branches</u>.
      A   B   C

NONE
25. Ⓐ Ⓑ Ⓒ Ⓓ

Words with /ər/ and /əl/

Pretest Directions

Fold back the paper along the dotted line. Use the blanks to write each word as it is read aloud. When you finish the test, unfold the paper. Use the list at the right to correct any spelling mistakes. Practice the words you missed for the Posttest.

To Parents

Here are the results of your child's weekly spelling Pretest. You can help your child study for the Posttest by following these simple steps for each word on the word list:

1. Read the word to your child.

2. Have your child write the word, saying each letter as it is written.

3. Say each letter of the word as your child checks the spelling.

4. If a mistake has been made, have your child read each letter of the correctly spelled word aloud, and then repeat steps 1-3.

1. _____	1. dinner
2. _____	2. signal
3. _____	3. fiddle
4. _____	4. favor
5. _____	5. collar
6. _____	6. handle
7. _____	7. summer
8. _____	8. travel
9. _____	9. metal
10. _____	10. motor
11. _____	11. cellar
12. _____	12. barrel
13. _____	13. center
14. _____	14. sailor
15. _____	15. stumble

Challenge Words

_____	accept
_____	equipment
_____	invisible
_____	perform
_____	talented

Words with /ər/ and /əl/

Using the Word Study Steps

1. LOOK at the word.

2. SAY the word aloud.

3. STUDY the letters in the word.

4. WRITE the word.

5. CHECK the word.
   Did you spell the word right?
   If not, go back to step 1.

Spelling Tip

Divide the word into syllables.
Example:

sum mer

fa vor

X the Word

Put an X on the word that does not match the pattern.

collar	hollow	dollar	cellar
dinner	summer	center	fiddle
barrel	favor	motor	sailor
travel	barrel	camel	metal
signal	metal	oral	mailer
stumble	bubble	favor	tumble
fiddle	handle	bundle	camel

To Parents or Helpers:
    Using the Word Study Steps above as your child comes across any new words will help him or her spell well.
Review the steps as you both go over this week's spelling words.
    Go over the Spelling Tip with your child. Ask your child to divide the other spelling words into syllables.
    Help your child find and circle the spelling words in the puzzle.

McGraw-Hill School Division

Words with /ər/ and /əl/

dinner	favor	summer	motor	center
signal	collar	travel	cellar	sailor
fiddle	handle	metal	barrel	stumble

Pattern Power!

Write the spelling words for each of these spelling patterns.

/ər/ spelled er

1. _____
2. _____
3. _____

/ər/ spelled ar

4. _____
5. _____

/ər/ spelled or

6. _____
7. _____
8. _____

/əl/ spelled le

9. _____
10. _____
11. _____

/əl/ spelled el

12. _____
13. _____

/əl/ spelled al

14. _____
15. _____

Syllable Patterns

How a word is divided into syllables may depend on whether the vowel in the first part of the word is long or short. Divide the following spelling words into syllables:

dinner

16. _____

collar

17. _____

favor

18. _____

signal

19. _____

motor

20. _____

Words with /ər/ and /əl/

dinner	favor	summer	motor	center
signal	collar	travel	cellar	sailor
fiddle	handle	metal	barrel	stumble

Finish the Sentence

Complete each sentence below using a spelling word.

1. The _____ returned from his long sea voyage.

2. Dorothy hid in her _____ when the tornado struck.

3. One player stood in the _____ of the circle.

4. Oil is measured and sold by the _____.

5. It was fun to _____, but I'm glad to be home.

6. The old toys were made of wood and _____.

7. I like to go swimming and hiking during _____ vacation.

8. I always eat Thanksgiving _____ at my grandmother's.

9. When I point at you, that will be your _____ to begin.

10. The model airplane was powered by a tiny _____.

Definitions

Write the spelling word that matches the definition.

11. a stringed instrument   _____

12. start to fall   _____

13. a friendly act   _____

14. something to hold on to   _____

15. part of the shirt around your neck   _____

McGraw-Hill School Division

Words with /ər/ and /əl/

Proofreading Paragraph

There are five spelling mistakes in the list below. Circle each misspelled word. Write the words correctly on the lines below.

Things to do this summer:

Learn to cook food for dinnir

Practice piano and fiddel

Travle to my uncle's house

Do a faver for a friend

Sew coller button on my blue shirt

Teach dog hand signel for a new trick

1. _____

2. _____

3. _____

4. _____

5. _____

6. _____

Writing Activity

Write a list of things you might enjoy doing inside on a rainy day. Use at least four spelling words.

_____

_____

_____

_____

_____

Words with /ər/ and /əl/

Look at the words in each set. One word in each set is spelled correctly.
Use a pencil to color in the circle in front of that word. Before you begin,
look at the sample sets of words. Sample A has been done for you.
Do Sample B by yourself. When you are sure you know what to do,
you may go on with the rest of the page.

Sample A
- Ⓐ middel
- Ⓑ midle
- ⬤ middle
- Ⓓ middal

Sample B
- Ⓔ turtel
- Ⓕ turtle
- Ⓖ tertel
- Ⓗ tertle

1.
- Ⓐ signel
- Ⓑ signle
- Ⓒ signil
- Ⓓ signal

2.
- Ⓔ fayvor
- Ⓕ favor
- Ⓖ faivor
- Ⓗ favore

3.
- Ⓐ handle
- Ⓑ handel
- Ⓒ handal
- Ⓓ handil

4.
- Ⓔ travle
- Ⓕ traval
- Ⓖ travel
- Ⓗ travile

5.
- Ⓐ moter
- Ⓑ motor
- Ⓒ mouter
- Ⓓ motar

6.
- Ⓔ barrel
- Ⓕ barrle
- Ⓖ barril
- Ⓗ barral

7.
- Ⓐ sailer
- Ⓑ sailar
- Ⓒ salor
- Ⓓ sailor

8.
- Ⓔ dinnar
- Ⓕ dinner
- Ⓖ dinnir
- Ⓗ dinar

9.
- Ⓐ fiddle
- Ⓑ fiddel
- Ⓒ fiddile
- Ⓓ fidle

10.
- Ⓔ coller
- Ⓕ collor
- Ⓖ collir
- Ⓗ collar

11.
- Ⓐ sumer
- Ⓑ summer
- Ⓒ summar
- Ⓓ summir

12.
- Ⓔ metle
- Ⓕ metel
- Ⓖ metal
- Ⓗ mettal

13.
- Ⓐ cellar
- Ⓑ celler
- Ⓒ cellor
- Ⓓ sellar

14.
- Ⓔ centar
- Ⓕ sentir
- Ⓖ centir
- Ⓗ center

15.
- Ⓐ stumple
- Ⓑ stumbil
- Ⓒ stumble
- Ⓓ stumbel

McGraw-Hill School Division

Words with Silent Letters

Pretest Directions

Fold back the paper along the dotted line. Use the blanks to write each word as it is read aloud. When you finish the test, unfold the paper. Use the list at the right to correct any spelling mistakes. Practice the words you missed for the Posttest.

To Parents

Here are the results of your child's weekly spelling Pretest. You can help your child study for the Posttest by following these simple steps for each word on the word list:

1. Read the word to your child.

2. Have your child write the word, saying each letter as it is written.

3. Say each letter of the word as your child checks the spelling.

4. If a mistake has been made, have your child read each letter of the correctly spelled word aloud, and then repeat steps 1-3.

1. _____ 1. wrong
2. _____ 2. known
3. _____ 3. daylight
4. _____ 4. comb
5. _____ 5. palm
6. _____ 6. knock
7. _____ 7. whole
8. _____ 8. frightening
9. _____ 9. limb
10. _____ 10. folk
11. _____ 11. wrinkle
12. _____ 12. knife
13. _____ 13. calf
14. _____ 14. crumb
15. _____ 15. height

Challenge Words

_____ bitter
_____ crystal
_____ gripped
_____ kingdom
_____ vanished

Words with Silent Letters

Using the Word Study Steps

1. **LOOK** at the word.

2. **SAY** the word aloud.

3. **STUDY** the letters in the word.

4. **WRITE** the word.

5. **CHECK** the word.
   Did you spell the word right?
   If not, go back to step 1.

Spelling Tip

Change the way you say a word to yourself to help with the spelling.

Example:

knife = /knīf/ Think of a related word to help you spell a word with a silent letter or a hard-to-hear sound.

Example:

     crumb, crumble

Circle the Rhyming Word

Circle the word that rhymes with the word in dark type.

crumb	comb	thumb	limb
palm	calm	folk	calf
knock	known	knife	rock
whole	whale	bowl	which
folk	tuck	soak	knife
calf	call	safe	half
height	weight	sight	mate
wrong	song	wrap	wrinkle
daylight	lightning	sunlight	frightening

To Parents or Helpers:

    Using the Word Study Steps above as your child comes across any new words will help him or her spell well. Review the steps as you both go over this week's spelling words.

    Go over each Spelling Tip with your child. Help him or her find other words that match the examples.

    Help your child find and circle the word that rhymes with the word in dark type.

McGraw-Hill School Division

Words with Silent Letters

wrong	comb	whole	folk	calf
known	palm	frightening	wrinkle	crumb
daylight	knock	limb	knife	height

Pattern Power!

Write the list words that have each silent letter.

k

1. _____

2. _____

3. _____

w

4. _____

5. _____

6. _____

l

7. _____

8. _____

9. _____

b

10. _____

11. _____

12. _____

gh

13. _____

14. _____

15. _____

Words within Words

Write the spelling word that contains the small word.

16. day _____

17. ink _____

18. own _____

19. eight _____

20. fright _____

Words with Silent Letters

wrong	comb	whole	folk	calf
known	palm	frightening	wrinkle	crumb
daylight	knock	limb	knife	height

Part of the Group

Read the heading for each group of words. Then add the spelling word that belongs in each group.

Baby Animals

1. puppy, lamb, _____

Things to Eat With

2. fork, spoon, _____

Tree Parts

3. trunk, root, _____

Parts of a Hand

4. wrist, finger, _____

Ways of Measuring Something **Things You Do with a Door**

5. length, width, _____

6. slam, open, _____

Things Used for Grooming

7. soap, toothbrush, _____

The Same or Opposite?

Write the spelling word that has the opposite meaning as the word below.

8. darkness _____

9. unknown _____

10. right _____

Write the spelling word that has the same meaning as the word or phrase.

11. small fold _____

12. small piece _____

13. people _____

14. incomplete _____

Challenge Extension: Have students draw pictures to illustrate challenge words. Students may exchange pictures with partner and guess the words.

170

Book 3.2/Unit 3
Two Bad Ants 14

McGraw-Hill School Division

Words with Silent Letters

Proofreading Paragraph

There are six spelling mistakes in the paragraph below. Circle each misspelled word. Write the words correctly on the lines below.

    This whole morning was horrible! If I had knoun so many things were going to go rawng, I would have shut out the daylite and gone right back to sleep! First, I dropped my cohm behind the table. When I made toast, I got crums all over the floor. Next, my favorite shirt had a big wrinkel in it. Wish me better luck tonight.

1. _____   2. _____   3. _____

4. _____   5. _____   6. _____

Writing Activity

Have you ever had a really bad day? If not, imagine what a really bad day might be like. Describe it on the lines below. Use four spelling words.

_____

_____

_____

_____

_____

Words with Silent Letters

Look at the words in each set. One word in each set is spelled correctly.
Use a pencil to color in the circle in front of that word. Before you begin,
look at the sample sets of words. Sample A has been done for you.
Do Sample B by yourself. When you are sure you know what to do,
you may go on with the rest of the page.

Sample A
- Ⓐ nis
- Ⓑ nys
- Ⓒ nyce
- Ⓓ **nice**

Sample B
- Ⓔ aloan
- Ⓕ alone
- Ⓖ alon
- Ⓗ aloane

1.
- Ⓐ hite
- Ⓑ hight
- Ⓒ height
- Ⓓ hyte

2.
- Ⓔ rong
- Ⓕ wrong
- Ⓖ rongh
- Ⓗ wronge

3.
- Ⓐ kohm
- Ⓑ combe
- Ⓒ comb
- Ⓓ caumb

4.
- Ⓔ noc
- Ⓕ knok
- Ⓖ nok
- Ⓗ knock

5.
- Ⓐ whoole
- Ⓑ whole
- Ⓒ whol
- Ⓓ hoole

6.
- Ⓔ lim
- Ⓕ limbe
- Ⓖ limb
- Ⓗ llimb

7.
- Ⓐ wrinckle
- Ⓑ rinkle
- Ⓒ wrinkle
- Ⓓ rincle

8.
- Ⓔ caph
- Ⓕ caf
- Ⓖ calph
- Ⓗ calf

9.
- Ⓐ daylite
- Ⓑ daylight
- Ⓒ dailight
- Ⓓ daylife

10.
- Ⓔ known
- Ⓕ knone
- Ⓖ nown
- Ⓗ knoon

11.
- Ⓐ pawmb
- Ⓑ pam
- Ⓒ palm
- Ⓓ pawm

12.
- Ⓔ krumb
- Ⓕ crum
- Ⓖ crumb
- Ⓗ crulm

13.
- Ⓐ fritening
- Ⓑ frightining
- Ⓒ frigtening
- Ⓓ frightening

14.
- Ⓔ foke
- Ⓕ fowlk
- Ⓖ folk
- Ⓗ folke

15.
- Ⓐ knif
- Ⓑ knife
- Ⓒ nighf
- Ⓓ nife

McGraw-Hill School Division

Homophones

Pretest Directions

Fold back the paper along the dotted line. Use the blanks to write each word as it is read aloud. When you finish the test, unfold the paper. Use the list at the right to correct any spelling mistakes. Practice the words you missed for the Posttest.

To Parents

Here are the results of your child's weekly spelling Pretest. You can help your child study for the Posttest by following these simple steps for each word on the word list:

1. Read the word to your child.

2. Have your child write the word, saying each letter as it is written.

3. Say each letter of the word as your child checks the spelling.

4. If a mistake has been made, have your child read each letter of the correctly spelled word aloud, and then repeat steps 1-3.

1. _____	1. ate
2. _____	2. meet
3. _____	3. eighth
4. _____	4. one
5. _____	5. so
6. _____	6. won
7. _____	7. meat
8. _____	8. sew
9. _____	9. to
10. _____	10. ant
11. _____	11. too
12. _____	12. do
13. _____	13. aunt
14. _____	14. two
15. _____	15. due

Challenge Words

_____ brain

_____ communicate

_____ social

_____ solve

_____ subject

Homophones

Using the Word Study Steps

1. LOOK at the word.

2. SAY the word aloud.

3. STUDY the letters in the word.

4. WRITE the word.

5. CHECK the word.
   Did you spell the word right?
   If not, go back to step 1.

Crossword Puzzle

Write the spelling word that best matches each clue. Put the spelling words in the boxes that start with the same number.

Crossword Clues

ACROSS

3. I went ____ the zoo.

5. Your parent's sister is your ____.

3. I will ____ my chores.

4. Let's ____ at school at 9 a.m.

9. I am only ____ person, but I am a person

DOWN

1. I like her and ____ does Abe.

2. I ____ the race.

3. The number that is one more than one is ____.

4. I will ____ on the button.

5. I ____ lunch early today.

6. I went to the zoo ____.

7. The rent is ____ on the first of the month.

Spelling Tip

• Learn common homophones such as **ate** and **eight** and make sure you have used the correct homophone in your writing.

• Use the spell-check in the computer, but read your writing carefully, too. The computer can't tell if you used a wrong words, such as *your* instead of *you're* or *it's* instead of *its*.

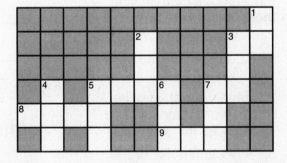

To Parents or Helpers:

Using the Word Study Steps above as your child comes across any new words will help him or her spell well. Review the steps as you both go over this week's spelling words.

Go over each Spelling Tip with your child. Ask if he or she knows other common homophones and can use each correctly. Also help your child use the spell-check in the computer.

Help your child solve the crossword puzzle.

McGraw-Hill School Division

Homophones

ate	one	meat	ant	aunt
meet	so	sew	too	two
eight	won	to	do	due

Homophones are words that sound alike but have different spellings and different meanings. Write the spelling words that are homophones on the lines below.

1. eight _____

2. meet _____

3. one _____

4. so _____

5. two _____

6. ant _____

7. do _____

Which spelling words are numbers?

8. _____ **9.** _____ **10.** _____

Write the spelling words that have the spelling patterns below.

short a	**long e**	**long o**
11. _____	**12.** _____	**13.** _____
14. _____	**15.** _____	**16.** _____

Write the spelling words that have only two letters. Circle the spelling word that doesn't rhyme with the other two.

17. _____ **18.** _____ **19.** _____

Homophones

ate	one	meat	ant	aunt
meet	so	sew	too	two
eight	won	to	do	due

Homophones are words that sound alike but have different spellings and different meanings. In each sentence below, a homophone is used incorrectly. Circle the incorrect homophone and write the correct homophone on the line following the sentence.

1. No one knew what to due. _____

2. We decided to meat at Stella's house. _____

3. Are you the won who called? _____

4. She is visiting her ant and uncle this weekend. _____

5. Do to the storm, there was no school today. _____

6. They eight lunch at noon. _____

7. My brother had meet and potatoes for supper. _____

8. I would make my own clothes if I knew how to so. _____

9. Which team one the football game? _____

10. Only to of us knew the answer. _____

11. He studied hard sew that he could pass the test. _____

12. You can't sleep late and go out for breakfast two! _____

13. The meeting ended at ate o'clock. _____

14. If you want too go, you have to start getting ready now. _____

15. Try not to step on that aunt! _____

Challenge Extension: Have students scramble the letters in the challenge words and exchange with a partner.

176

Book 3.2/Unit 3
Do Animals Think? | 15

Homophones

Proofreading Paragraph

There are six spelling mistakes in the paragraph below. Circle each misspelled word. Write the words correctly on the lines below.

The play was supposed to begin at eigt o'clock. Before the show, we ait dinner at a fancy restaurant. I ordered spaghetti with maet sauce. My ahnt wanted spaghetti too. "Two orders of spaghetti," said the waiter. My uncle was supposed to meete us at the restaurant. Doo to a traffic jam, he arrived at the theater late and missed Act One.

1. _____ 2. _____ 3. _____

4. _____ 5. _____ 6. _____

Writing Activity

What's your favorite play, movie, or television show? Tell about it in a few sentences. Use four spelling words in your description.

_____

_____

_____

_____

_____

Homophones

Look at the words in each set. One word in each set is spelled correctly.
Use a pencil to color in the circle in front of that word. Before you begin,
look at the sample sets of words. Sample A has been done for you.
Do Sample B by yourself. When you are sure you know what to do,
you may go on with the rest of the page.

Sample A
- Ⓐ whole
- Ⓑ wole
- Ⓒ whol
- Ⓓ hol

Sample B
- Ⓔ accept
- Ⓕ except
- Ⓖ axept
- Ⓗ exxept

1. Ⓐ sewe
   Ⓑ sowe
   Ⓒ soo
   Ⓓ sew

2. Ⓔ two
   Ⓕ tiw
   Ⓖ twoo
   Ⓗ tue

3. Ⓐ tiew
   Ⓑ too
   Ⓒ twoe
   Ⓓ tooe

4. Ⓔ dooe
   Ⓕ do
   Ⓖ deue
   Ⓗ diue

5. Ⓐ doo
   Ⓑ deu
   Ⓒ due
   Ⓓ dou

6. Ⓔ ant
   Ⓕ ahnt
   Ⓖ aint
   Ⓗ anit

7. Ⓐ aunte
   Ⓑ ante
   Ⓒ aunet
   Ⓓ aunt

8. Ⓔ tu
   Ⓕ to
   Ⓖ tue
   Ⓗ twu

9. Ⓐ wun
   Ⓑ wone
   Ⓒ wune
   Ⓓ one

10. Ⓔ maet
    Ⓕ meete
    Ⓖ meet
    Ⓗ maete

11. Ⓐ eigt
    Ⓑ eight
    Ⓒ eitgh
    Ⓓ egith

12. Ⓔ so
    Ⓕ sewe
    Ⓖ sowe
    Ⓗ soo

13. Ⓐ mit
    Ⓑ meete
    Ⓒ maet
    Ⓓ meat

14. Ⓔ wune
    Ⓕ wun
    Ⓖ won
    Ⓗ wone

15. Ⓐ ate
    Ⓑ ayte
    Ⓒ ayt
    Ⓓ atte

McGraw-Hill School Division

Words with Suffixes

Pretest Directions

Fold back the paper along the dotted line. Use the blanks to write each word as it is read aloud. When you finish the test, unfold the paper. Use the list at the right to correct any spelling mistakes. Practice the words you missed for the Posttest.

To Parents

Here are the results of your child's weekly spelling Pretest. You can help your child study for the Posttest by following these simple steps for each word on the word list:

1. Read the word to your child.

2. Have your child write the word, saying each letter as it is written.

3. Say each letter of the word as your child checks the spelling.

4. If a mistake has been made, have your child read each letter of the correctly spelled word aloud, and then repeat steps 1-3.

1. _____
2. _____
3. _____
4. _____
5. _____
6. _____
7. _____
8. _____
9. _____
10. _____
11. _____
12. _____
13. _____
14. _____
15. _____

1. wonderful
2. direction
3. sadly
4. comfortable
5. quietly
6. possession
7. useful
8. collection
9. valuable
10. invention
11. powerful
12. discussion
13. busily
14. expression
15. unbelievable

Challenge Words

_____   considering
_____   conversation
_____   hesitated
_____   interrupted
_____   seized

McGraw-Hill School Division

Words with Suffixes

Using the Word Study Steps

1. LOOK at the word.

2. SAY the word aloud.

3. STUDY the letters in the word.

4. WRITE the word.

5. CHECK the word.
   Did you spell the word right?
   If not, go back to step 1.

Spelling Tip

- Learn to spell prefixes and suffixes you use often in writing.

- When words in silent **e**, drop the **e** when adding an ending that begins with a vowel.
Example:
     value + able = valuable

- When a word ends with a consonant followed by **y**, change the **y** to **i** when adding any ending except endings that begin with **i**.
Example:
     busy + ly = busily

Find and Circle

Where are the spelling words?

```
w o n d e r f u l u n b e l i e v a b l e u s e f u l
c o m f o r t a b l e c o l l e c t i o n b u s i l y
i n v e n t i o n d i s c u s s i o n p o w e r f u l
e x p r e s s i o n n s a d l y p o s s e s s i o n q
u q u i e t l y f v a l u a b l e z d i r e c t i o n
```

To Parents or Helpers:
    Using the Word Study Steps above as your child comes across any new words will help him or her spell well. Review the steps as you both go over this week's spelling words.
    Go over each Spelling Tip with your child. Ask him or her find other words with prefixes and suffixes that often are used in writing. Help him or her find other words that match the examples.
    Help your child find and circle the spelling words in the puzzle.

Book 3.2/Unit 3
The Boast 15

Words with Suffixes

wonderful	comfortable	useful	invention	busily
direction	quietly	collection	powerful	expression
sadly	possession	valuable	discussion	unbelievable

Write the spelling words that end with each of these suffixes.

-ly   **-ful**   **-able**

1. _____   4. _____   7. _____

2. _____   5. _____   8. _____

3. _____   6. _____   9. _____

-tion   **-sion**

10. _____   13. _____

11. _____   14. _____

12. _____   15. _____

Words with Suffixes

wonderful	comfortable	useful	invention	busily
direction	quietly	collection	powerful	expression
sadly	possession	valuable	discussion	unbelievable

For each spelling word below write the base word. The first one is done for you.

1. wonderful   **wonder**

2. direction   _____

3. sadly   _____

4. comfortable   _____

5. quietly   _____

6. possession   _____

7. useful   _____

8. collection   _____

9. valuable   _____

10. invention   _____

11. powerful   _____

12. discussion   _____

13. busily   _____

14. expression   _____

15. unbelievable   _____

Which of the above spelling words changes y to i when adding a suffix?

16. _____

Which words drop e when adding a suffix?

17. _____   18. _____

Challenge Extension: Have students write fill-in sentences with challenge words and exchange with a partner.

Book 3.2/Unit 3
The Boast 18

McGraw-Hill School Division

Words with Suffixes

Proofreading Paragraph

There are six spelling mistakes in the selection below. Circle each misspelled word. Write the words correctly on the lines below.

Collecting stamps is a wundaful hobby. Saddly, some people think it takes a lot of money to start a stamp colection. All you really need are a few stamps and a comfurtable chair to sit in. Stamps don't have to be valuble to be interesting. It's unbeleevable how many different kinds of stamps there are. So join a stamp club!

1. _____   2. _____   3. _____

4. _____   5. _____   6. _____

Writing Activity

Do you have a hobby? If not, is there a hobby you would be interested in learning more about? Describe a hobby that you find interesting. Use four spelling words in your description.

_____

_____

_____

_____

Words with Suffixes

Look at the words in each set. One word in each set is spelled correctly.
Use a pencil to color in the circle in front of that word. Before you begin,
look at the sample sets of words. Sample A has been done for you.
Do Sample B by yourself. When you are sure you know what to do,
you may go on with the rest of the page.

Sample A
- Ⓐ carfuly
- Ⓑ kerfuly
- Ⓒ karefully
- ⬤ carefully

Sample B
- Ⓔ eihgt
- Ⓕ eight
- Ⓖ eigt
- Ⓗ eaight

1.
- Ⓐ unbeleivable
- Ⓑ unbeleevable
- Ⓒ unbelievable
- Ⓓ unbeliefable

6.
- Ⓔ invension
- Ⓕ invention
- Ⓖ invenshun
- Ⓗ invenshion

11.
- Ⓐ kwietly
- Ⓑ quietly
- Ⓒ quitally
- Ⓓ quitely

2.
- Ⓔ expreshion
- Ⓕ expression
- Ⓖ expresion
- Ⓗ exprettion

7.
- Ⓐ valuable
- Ⓑ valuble
- Ⓒ valueable
- Ⓓ valubel

12.
- Ⓔ comfortable
- Ⓕ comfortble
- Ⓖ comfertable
- Ⓗ comfurtable

3.
- Ⓐ busyly
- Ⓑ bizily
- Ⓒ busly
- Ⓓ busily

8.
- Ⓔ collecttion
- Ⓕ colleksion
- Ⓖ collekshun
- Ⓗ collection

13.
- Ⓐ sadely
- Ⓑ saddily
- Ⓒ saddly
- Ⓓ sadly

4.
- Ⓔ discussion
- Ⓕ discushun
- Ⓖ discusion
- Ⓗ discution

9.
- Ⓐ usefull
- Ⓑ useful
- Ⓒ usful
- Ⓓ usfull

14.
- Ⓔ direcktion
- Ⓕ durection
- Ⓖ direction
- Ⓗ direktion

5.
- Ⓐ powirful
- Ⓑ powurfull
- Ⓒ powerful
- Ⓓ powerfull

10.
- Ⓔ posesion
- Ⓕ posession
- Ⓖ possession
- Ⓗ posseshun

15.
- Ⓐ wunderfull
- Ⓑ wunderful
- Ⓒ wonderfull
- Ⓓ wonderful

McGraw-Hill School Division

Words from Social Studies

Pretest Directions

Fold back the paper along the dotted line. Use the blanks to write each word as it is read aloud. When you finish the test, unfold the paper. Use the list at the right to correct any spelling mistakes. Practice the words you missed for the Posttest.

To Parents

Here are the results of your child's weekly spelling Pretest. You can help your child study for the Posttest by following these simple steps for each word on the word list:

1. Read the word to your child.

2. Have your child write the word, saying each letter as it is written.

3. Say each letter of the word as your child checks the spelling.

4. If a mistake has been made, have your child read each letter of the correctly spelled word aloud, and then repeat steps 1-3.

1.	_____	1. coast
2.	_____	2. valley
3.	_____	3. port
4.	_____	4. outdoors
5.	_____	5. wildlife
6.	_____	6. harmed
7.	_____	7. safe
8.	_____	8. bay
9.	_____	9. island
10.	_____	10. country
11.	_____	11. gulf
12.	_____	12. migrate
13.	_____	13. forests
14.	_____	14. continent
15.	_____	15. mainland

Challenge Words

_____ crates

_____ loops

_____ rescuers

_____ starve

_____ strip

McGraw-Hill School Division

Words from Social Studies

Using the Word Study Steps

1. LOOK at the word.

2. SAY the word aloud.

3. STUDY the letters in the word.

4. WRITE the word.

5. CHECK the word.
   Did you spell the word right?
   If not, go back to step 1.

| **Spelling Tip** |
| Look for chunks or smaller words that help you remember the spelling of a word. Example: out + doors = outdoors |

Word Scramble

Unscramble each set of letters to make a spelling word.

1. ropt _____

2. ndmnliaa _____

3. soact _____

4. feas _____

5. flug _____

6. ayb _____

7. tyrncuo _____

8. dstorouo _____

9. defiiwll _____

10. tcnnioetn _____

11. rossetf _____

12. dheamr _____

13. llvyae _____

14. lsdnai _____

15. gmtarei _____

To Parents or Helpers:
   Using the Word Study Steps above as your child comes across any new words will help him or her spell well. Review the steps as you both go over this week's spelling words.
   Go over each Spelling Tip with your child. Help him or her find helpful chunks or smaller words in other new words.
   Help your child unscramble the letters to make spelling words.

McGraw-Hill School Division

Words from Social Studies

coast	outdoors	safe	country	forests
valley	wildlife	bay	gulf	continent
port	harmed	island	migrate	mainland

Order, Please!

Write the spelling words in alphabetical order.

1. _____ 2. _____ 3. _____

4. _____ 5. _____ 6. _____

7. _____ 8. _____ 9. _____

10. _____ 11. _____ 12. _____

13. _____ 14. _____ 15. _____

Words Within Words

Write the spelling words that contain these smaller words.

16. out _____

17. life _____

18. harm _____

19. land _____ 20. _____

Words from Social Studies

coast	outdoors	safe	country	forests
valley	wildlife	bay	gulf	continent
port	harmed	island	migrate	mainland

Crossword

Complete the crossword puzzle. Write the spelling word that fits each clue.

Across

3. hurt

5. body of water, usually larger than a bay

6. flat land between hills

7. wooded areas

Down

1. animals

2. not in danger

4. move to a different place

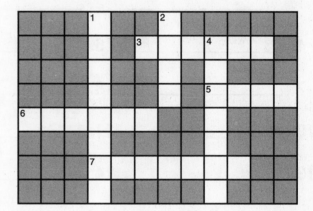

Compound Words

A compound word is made up of two or more smaller words. Connect the words to form other compound words.

8. in   cat

9. wild   bell

10. door   side

Words from Social Studies

Proofreading Paragraph

There are six spelling mistakes in the paragraph below. Circle each misspelled word. Write the words correctly on the lines below.

We were really going from Europe to the New World! I knew I would miss the beautiful vallie and lush green forists of my childhood home. We traveled owtdoors for many days. Finally, we reached the coaste. A great sailing ship was waiting for us at the porte.

"What will the New World be like?" I asked. My father shook his head. The new contanent was as much a mystery to him as it was to me.

1. _____ 2. _____ 3. _____

4. _____ 5. _____ 6. _____

Writing Activity

It can be very frightening to leave your home and move to a new place with different people and strange ways of life. Imagine that you live in the distant future. Your family has decided to leave Earth and live on another planet. Write a few sentences that describe how you feel on leaving Earth. Use four spelling words.

_____

_____

_____

_____

_____

_____

Words from Social Studies

Look at the words in each set. One word in each set is spelled correctly.
Use a pencil to color in the circle in front of that word. Before you begin,
look at the sample sets of words. Sample A has been done for you.
Do Sample B by yourself. When you are sure you know what to do,
you may go on with the rest of the page.

Sample A
Ⓐ classroom
Ⓑ klassroom
Ⓒ clasroom
Ⓓ classrheum

Sample B
Ⓔ enything
Ⓕ anythang
Ⓖ anything
Ⓗ innyting

1. Ⓐ vallie
   Ⓑ valley
   Ⓒ vally
   Ⓓ valey

2. Ⓔ outdors
   Ⓕ outdores
   Ⓖ outdoors
   Ⓗ owtdoors

3. Ⓐ harmed
   Ⓑ harmd
   Ⓒ hermed
   Ⓓ hormed

4. Ⓔ baye
   Ⓕ baie
   Ⓖ bay
   Ⓗ bae

5. Ⓐ countrie
   Ⓑ cauntry
   Ⓒ countery
   Ⓓ country

6. Ⓔ migrate
   Ⓕ migraite
   Ⓖ mygrate
   Ⓗ migrait

7. Ⓐ faurests
   Ⓑ forests
   Ⓒ farests
   Ⓓ forasts

8. Ⓔ maineland
   Ⓕ maynland
   Ⓖ mainland
   Ⓗ mainlend

9. Ⓐ continent
   Ⓑ cantinent
   Ⓒ continant
   Ⓓ contanent

10. Ⓔ gulph
    Ⓕ gulfe
    Ⓖ golfe
    Ⓗ gulf

11. Ⓐ iland
    Ⓑ island
    Ⓒ ilande
    Ⓓ islande

12. Ⓔ saphe
    Ⓕ sayf
    Ⓖ saif
    Ⓗ safe

13. Ⓐ wildlife
    Ⓑ wilelife
    Ⓒ wildlyfe
    Ⓓ wyldlife

14. Ⓔ purt
    Ⓕ porte
    Ⓖ port
    Ⓗ puert

15. Ⓐ coste
    Ⓑ caust
    Ⓒ cohst
    Ⓓ coast

McGraw-Hill School Division

Book 3.2/Unit 3 Review Test

Read each sentence. If an underlined word is spelled wrong, fill in the circle that
goes with that word. If no word is spelled wrong, fill in the circle below NONE.
Read Sample A, and do Sample B.

A. He'll teach you to play the fidle.
A   B   C

                                                                   NONE
A. Ⓐ   Ⓑ   ●   Ⓓ

B. Millions watch the sunsete in the city.
     E   F   G

                                                                   NONE
B. Ⓔ   Ⓕ   Ⓖ   Ⓗ

1. There were eight islands in that country.
            A   B   C

                                                                    NONE
1. Ⓐ   Ⓑ   Ⓒ   Ⓓ

2. They migrate to the vallie in the summer.
         E   F   G

                                                                     NONE
2. Ⓔ   Ⓕ   Ⓖ   Ⓗ

3. We need an island breeze at the height of the summer.
                 A   B   C

                                                            NONE
3. Ⓐ   Ⓑ   Ⓒ   Ⓓ

4. She wan a fiddle in camp this summer.
        E   F   G

                                                                    NONE
4. Ⓔ   Ⓕ   Ⓖ   Ⓗ

5. I hear a nok on the cellar door.
     A   B   C

                                                                     NONE
5. Ⓐ   Ⓑ   Ⓒ   Ⓓ

6. My aunt one the game.
       E   F   G

                                                                     NONE
6. Ⓔ   Ⓕ   Ⓖ   Ⓗ

7. The metal barrel will be yusefull.
         A   B   C

                                                                   NONE
7. Ⓐ   Ⓑ   Ⓒ   Ⓓ

8. That the crook won is wrong and unbelevable.
                E   F   G

                                                                  NONE
8. Ⓐ   Ⓑ   Ⓒ   Ⓓ

9. We like to fiddle on a country summer night.
              A   B   C

                                                                    NONE
9. Ⓔ   Ⓕ   Ⓖ   Ⓗ

10. The pickle barell is due from the mainland today.
               E   F   G

                                                                    NONE
10. Ⓔ   Ⓕ   Ⓖ   Ⓗ

Go on ➡

11. In <u>sumer</u>, the deer <u>migrate</u> to a new <u>valley</u>.　11. Ⓐ Ⓑ Ⓒ Ⓓ
　　　A　　　　　　B　　　　　　　　C　　　　　　　　　　　　　　　　　　NONE

12. You used the <u>wrong</u> thread to <u>so</u> my <u>aunt's</u> dress.　12. Ⓔ Ⓕ Ⓖ Ⓗ
　　　　　　　E　　　　　　F　　　G　　　　　　　　　　　　　　　　NONE

13. I <u>won</u> a doll <u>collekshin</u> from all over the <u>country</u>.　13. Ⓐ Ⓑ Ⓒ Ⓓ
　　A　　　　　B　　　　　　　　　　　　C　　　　　　　　　　　　NONE

14. The <u>barrel</u> and the <u>fiddle</u> are kept in the <u>seller</u>.　14. Ⓔ Ⓕ Ⓖ Ⓗ
　　　　E　　　　　　　F　　　　　　　　　　G　　　　　　　　　NONE

15. The <u>mouse</u> is <u>sadly</u> looking for a <u>crumm</u> to eat.　15. Ⓐ Ⓑ Ⓒ Ⓓ
　　　　A　　　　B　　　　　　　　　C　　　　　　　　　　　　NONE

16. Our <u>ant</u> is <u>due</u> to arrive in this <u>country</u>.　16. Ⓔ Ⓕ Ⓖ Ⓗ
　　　E　　　F　　　　　　　　　　G　　　　　　　　　　　　NONE

17. <u>Knock</u> on your head <u>eight</u> times in this <u>ffok</u> dance.　17. Ⓐ Ⓑ Ⓒ Ⓓ
　　A　　　　　　　　　B　　　　　　　　C　　　　　　　　　NONE

18. Every <u>summer</u> we leave <u>mainland</u> for an <u>iland</u>.　18. Ⓔ Ⓕ Ⓖ Ⓗ
　　　　E　　　　　　　　F　　　　　　G　　　　　　　　　NONE

19. What a <u>usefull</u> <u>collection</u> of <u>folk</u> sayings!　19. Ⓐ Ⓑ Ⓒ Ⓓ
　　　　A　　　　　B　　　　C　　　　　　　　　　　　　　NONE

20. We ate <u>eight</u> <u>krum</u> cakes this <u>summer</u>.　20. Ⓔ Ⓕ Ⓖ Ⓗ
　　　　E　　F　　　　　　　G　　　　　　　　　　　　NONE

21. <u>Do</u> to the <u>migration</u>, the <u>country</u> grew.　21. Ⓐ Ⓑ Ⓒ Ⓓ
　　A　　　　　B　　　　　C　　　　　　　　　　　　　NONE

22. The <u>metal</u> <u>cellar</u> door groaned <u>sadly</u> when opened.　22. Ⓔ Ⓕ Ⓖ Ⓗ
　　　　E　　　F　　　　　　　　G　　　　　　　　　　NONE

23. I <u>won</u> a necklace with <u>eight</u> <u>metal</u> charms.　23. Ⓐ Ⓑ Ⓒ Ⓓ
　　A　　　　　　　　　B　　　C　　　　　　　　　　　　NONE

24. This <u>summer</u> I grew <u>eight</u> inches in <u>hight</u>.　24. Ⓔ Ⓕ Ⓖ Ⓗ
　　　　E　　　　　　　F　　　　　　　G　　　　　　　　NONE

25. <u>Fiddle</u> dee dee is a <u>folk</u> <u>expresion</u>.　25. Ⓐ Ⓑ Ⓒ Ⓓ
　　A　　　　　　　　B　　　C